Hi, I'm Hungry

RECIPES INSPIRED BY EVERYDAY MOMENTS

Written + Photographed by

Melissa Santell

Dedicated to my wonderful family.
You've inspired me in more ways
than I can say.

Published in the United States by FoodxFeels.

ISBN 978-0-578-64246-8

Cover design by Jessie Stehlik

Book design by Melissa Santell

Edited by Jenna Rimensnyder

Headshots by Kait Clarke + Jessie Stehlik

First Edition

FOOD x Feels

Rainbow Butter Cookies
PAGE 171

Introduction

I've always refused to be put in a box. You know, the kind that comes with some sort of weird ownership over who or what you are.

In 7th grade I was labeled as a "skater," solely because I accessorized my black nails and pink Phat Farm sneakers with a leather studded belt. Even though I've never owned a skateboard.

In 9th grade, I was the girl who routinely ate chocolate chip cookies during first period homeroom and reheated Pasta e Fagioli in the lunchroom microwave. Then, I became the 4'11" chick who somehow managed to make it on the volleyball team, while simultaneously finding time to play the clarinet in marching band. Oh, and I sang the hell out of my Les Miserables "On My Own" solo at the Market Street choir concert, too.

By the time I graduated from high school, I was an enigma. Perfectly unboxable, and I fucking loved it. Because the freedom that comes with unapologetically being yourself is the most delicious magic you'll ever taste.

My relationship with food shares a similar story.

As a child, I regularly protested eggs and bacon for breakfast. My appetite took me to different, unconventional places. One that insisted on eating a can of Albacore tuna with sliced sharp cheddar cheese before 8 a.m. This meal was always paired with a tall glass of Hershey's chocolate milk poured over crushed ice. If you're reading this right now and cringing, you should know you're probably not alone.

As long as I was eating something relatively healthy, my parents were gracious enough to let me make my own decisions. Except that time I had the chickenpox and constructed one giant ball made entirely of Lucky Charms marshmallows. Rummaging through the red cardboard box to discard every piece of cereal was a project that took a commendable amount of patience for a six-year-old. But it was that kind of curiosity that led me to experiment with food at a wildly young age. The kitchen became a space for exploration, without boundaries.

It wasn't long before I was working at our local pizza shop, throwing pies in the air and wearing a very flattering veil of flour, basically at all times. I became the unofficial sous chef in our kitchen during holidays, and the one being asked to make trays of baked ziti for graduation parties. I couldn't learn enough about food then, and still, I never want to stop learning.

So, who am I today?

I'm the person who launched the very first food critic role for the campus newspaper at The University of Tampa. A woman who dedicated two years of her life to a luxury catering and events kitchen in Manhattan, marketing the company and sneaking bites of peanut butter gelato from the 10,000-square-foot commissary kitchen. Today, I'm a blogger who interviews James Beard Award-winning chefs, every chance I get. I photograph food, my own and others, and develop shareable recipes for clients. I work for myself in the food and beverage space and eat whatever I want, on any given occasion.

All of those moments serve as the inspiration behind this book. *Hi, I'm Hungry* is my interpretation of reinvented classics like Cannoli French Toast and French Onion Soup Flatbread, that refuse to let things stay as they are, and encourage them to evolve into whatever you want them to be. Because while there are rules in the kitchen, there is no limit to what you can create. I totally encourage you to scribble outside of my recipe lines and try your own version, too.

These recipes are approachable, use ingredients you likely already have in your kitchen and are stylistically categorized by everyday moments. You can, of course, cook or bake any of these recipes whenever they call out to you! I found myself wanting to give each one a relatable place and time, like 'what to eat when you're wildly hungover,' or 'recipes to upgrade your next dinner party.' This book exists to make eating (and cooking) fun and easy for you. I'm not a classically trained Le Cordon Bleu chef, and you don't have to be one either - just be yourself, you know?!

Growing up in an Italian family, our kitchen was always stocked with the best tins of

olive oil, fresh bunches of basil from the garden, heaping towers of tomatoes and all the ricotta cheese I could ever want. So, if you're feeling Italian undertones in these recipes, know that each one is full of love, family and endless conversations echoed by our hands.

I hope you find this book to be perfectly imperfect. It doesn't require a label. Just you, your kitchen and the people you love to feed.

MANGIA,

Melissa Santell

10 Cooking Commandments

1. Leftovers rule. More specifically, they're the perfect foundation for a frittata (page 53), and delicious when thrown into a green leafy salad. So, stop neglecting them, okay?

2. Garlic is the lifeblood of everything that is sacred in this book (and basically every savory recipe to date), so stock up. P.S. Don't hold back from using it because you're worried about your breath. Mints are a glorious invention.

3. Make all the recipes that scare you, overwhelm you and excite you. You'll be pleasantly surprised by the fun you'll have in the process. If you don't know where to start, whip up one of Grandma's Cheesecakes (page 184).

4. When baking, all ingredients should always be the same temperature. Most often, that means room temperature. Eggs, butter, milk; the whole lot. Highlight this commandment, rip this page out, frame it, hang it in your kitchen.

5. When in doubt, use a thermometer. Don't have one? I recommend OXO brand. The key temperatures to remember are: medium rare steak (135°F), chicken (165°F) and pork (145°F).Overcooked meat is not fun for anyone.

6. Don't feel imprisoned by the recipe. These recipes are designed to serve as creative guides for you to experiment in the kitchen. So, do exactly that. Seriously, I won't tell anyone if you secretly opt for avocado oil instead of olive oil.

7. When it comes to nuts, toast them. Drop them in a hot skillet or roast them in the oven on a baking sheet with a little sea salt. Toasting brings out the rich, aromatic personality of nuts. It also makes your house smell wonderful. You're welcome.

8. Homemade dressing triumphs over store-bought dressing. Every. Single. Time. There's no magical ratio for oil to vinegar, or fats to acidity. Make it at home and taste as you go; when you get it right, it's the ultimate form of satisfaction.

9. For ingredient modifications, there's no shame in using what you already have in your kitchen. I'll never ask you to make a frantic grocery store run for a special breed of $15 olives when you have a beautiful jar of Kalamatas sitting inside your fridge. With that being said, it's ideal to read recipes at least a day ahead of cooking so you can snag last minute ingredients, if you need them.

10. Shop at your local farmer's market as often as possible. I have a farm that I frequent and let me tell you, it's pretty cool to be friends with the chicken who lays your eggs.

Wait... make that 11 commandments. Lastly, make this experience FUN. So what if you're baking a self-pity cake? You're about to make the best damn cake ever and have an awesome time eating it by yourself, on your unbirthday. It's time to turn up the music, pop open a bottle of Cab Franc and making something amazing with your two bare hands.

YOUR FLA

WHEN YOU'RE CRAVING CHILDHOOD COMFORT FOOD

When I was 13 years old, all I wanted to do was grow up. You know, the age where you routinely start refusing a 9 p.m. bedtime and beg for a cell phone (that you'll never have to pay for). You crave independence, but expect your parents to cook a "well-balanced" dinner every night. And they do, because they don't have much of a choice. For a moment, it feels like you actually have the best of both worlds. Then suddenly without your permission, you become an adult.

This chapter exists to bring you back to simpler times and your favorite childhood food memories. While it's still 100% acceptable to devour a crust-less peanut butter & jelly sandwich at your desk, I can't wait to show you how to recreate those flavors in a "grown-up" way. Welcome to the world of edible nostalgia.

PB&J Meringues

Peanut butter and jelly is the heart of all childhood food memories. You know it, I know it, and every American who's ever carried a brown paper bag to school knows it.

As a kid, I knew that if my mother packed my lunch I wouldn't be subjected to a hot plate of slop from the lunch line. Full disclosure: the lunch ladies were modern day saints and I know the shitty food was not entirely their fault. While the other kids were busy swapping their "boring" PB&J's for turkey sandwiches, I was subconsciously doing research and development for this recipe. Clearly.

I hope it makes you feel like you're back in second grade, but sitting in an ergonomic chair at a Crate and Barrel desk. This one's for you!

Makes 15 Cookies.

4 egg whites, room temperature

1/8 teaspoon cream of tartar

Pinch of salt

3/4 cup fine sugar

1 teaspoon vanilla extract

1/3 cup smooth peanut butter

1/2 cup freeze-dried strawberries or blueberries, crushed finely

1. Preheat the oven to 200°F. Line two cookie sheets with parchment paper.

2. In a large bowl, use a standing or hand mixer to whisk together egg whites, cream of tartar and salt. Beat on medium-high speed until soft, white peaks form.

3. Add sugar to the mixture, one tablespoon at a time, beating until the sugar dissolves in between additions. You can test this by squeezing the mixture in between your fingers. If it's gritty, keep beating.

4. When all of the sugar has been added, mix in the vanilla, then continue to beat the egg whites until they are glossy and stiff, about 2-3 minutes. When you can hold the bowl upside down over your head and the mixture stays put, you're golden.

5. Drop small spoonfuls of peanut butter on top of the meringue. Use a rubber spatula to lightly fold the peanut butter into the mixture, creating silky swirls.

6. Use the spatula to create 3-inch nests of meringue on your prepared cookie sheets.

7. Bake for 1 ½ hours. Then, turn the oven off and let meringues cool completely before you remove them.

8. Once cooled, use a blender to crush the freeze dried berries. Sprinkle on top of meringues and voila! Fluffy clouds of PB+J.

I WISH
I Found You
SOONER, SO I COULD
Love You Longer

Cozy Tomato Soup

Tomato soup is arguably the most iconic soup of all time.

I have yet to decide if my love for it was inspired by Andy Warhol, or the fact that it was a household staple throughout my childhood. Regardless, it was the soup that was always there when I needed it, and only a can opener away.

This recipe makes a gorgeously creamy soup using freshly roasted cherry and Roma tomatoes. For a dairy-free version, skip the heavy cream and add coconut milk. No matter how you choose to enjoy it, it's best served with a buttery grilled cheese sandwich or garlicky

Makes 4 Servings.

ROASTED TOMATOES

3 pounds cherry tomatoes, roasted

5 roma tomatoes, quartered

2 carrots, halved + roasted

5 thyme sprigs

1 1/4 teaspoons sea salt

1 teaspoon black pepper

1/4 cup good olive oil (I love Filippo Berio)

SOUP

3 tablespoons olive oil

3 tablespoons butter

5 garlic cloves, roughly chopped

1 large shallot, minced

1/2 teaspoon of red pepper flakes

2 tablespoons tomato paste

1 quart chicken stock

1/2 cup heavy cream

1 teaspoon salt

1 cup basil leaves, torn

1. Preheat oven to 250°F.

2. Place tomatoes, carrots, thyme, sea salt, pepper and olive oil on a baking sheet. Shake the sheet to coat the ingredients in olive oil and seasoning. Roast for 2 1/2 - 3 hours. Remove from oven and set aside.

3. In a large heavy bottomed pot, melt butter and olive oil over medium heat. Add garlic, shallot and red pepper. Saute for 3-5 minutes until soft.

4. Mix in tomato paste and cook for 1 minute. Add roasted vegetables into the pot, followed by chicken stock. Simmer on low for 15-20 minutes.

5. Remove thyme sprigs, then use an immersion blender to purée the soup until it's velvety smooth.

6. Finish by stirring in heavy cream.

7. To serve, ladle into bowls and garnish with basil and a dollop of sour cream (optional).

Frozen Hot Chocolate

If you read the title of this recipe and thought to yourself, "why would I ever drink frozen hot chocolate?" Let me remind you that I'm a New Yorker gone Floridian. I should also tell you that this recipe doubles as a boozy frozen cocktail for your next holiday party and will be your new poolside partner in the middle of summer.

There's never a wrong time for frozen hot chocolate. Happy sipping!

Makes 4 Servings.

HOT CHOCOLATE

3 cups vanilla oat milk

1 1/2 cups chocolate chips, roughly chopped

2 teaspoons vanilla extract

2 shots of cassis liqueur

Hefty pinch of cinnamon

3-4 cups of ice

Vodka (optional)

Cocoa nibs + mini marshmallows, for garnish

WHIPPED CREAM

1/2 cup heavy cream, very cold

1 tablespoon confectioners' sugar

1/2 teaspoon vanilla extract

1. In a medium pan, heat milk over medium heat for 2-3 minutes. Do not let boil.

2. Remove from heat. Stir in chocolate chips, continuously stirring until they've melted, about 1-2 minutes.

3. Whisk in vanilla, cassis and a pinch of cinnamon. Set aside to cool.

4. Meanwhile, combine cold heavy whipping cream, vanilla and sugar in a large bowl. Use a stand or hand mixer to beat on high speed for 1 minute or until stiff peaks form. Don't over whip!

5. Once drink mixture has cooled, blend with ice. I recommend adding 1 cup of ice at a time, for full control over the consistency.

6. Pour frozen hot chocolate into a short glass. If adding vodka, swirl 1 shot into each serving. Top with whipped cream, cocoa nibs and marshmallows.

7. Serve and sip.

Old School Banana Bread

There were four words I consistently looked forward to as a teenager. While "I love you, Melissa" was definitely important, the words I'm actually referring to were, "the banana bread's ready!" Both famous for coming out of my mother's mouth, who perfected this recipe back when the Spice Girls were a thing.

I know there are a million ways to make a delicious loaf. Zucchini bread, pumpkin bread, garlic bread —bread gets around. The only bread in the world I'll never get tired of is this banana bread, because this recipe actually tastes like cake. It's fabulous with a slab of softened butter, or a glorious smear of peanut butter. You can even eat it with a scoop of vanilla ice cream, drizzled with caramel.

Makes 1 Loaf.

4 ripe bananas, peeled

1/3 cup unsalted butter, melted

3/4 cup sugar

1 egg, room temperature

1/8 cup maple syrup

1 teaspoon vanilla extract

2 cups flour

1 teaspoon baking soda

1/4 teaspoon salt

1. Preheat oven to 350°F.

2. Slice one banana in half, length-wise. In a medium sized bowl, use a standing or hand mixer to blend 3 and a half bananas and butter together on low speed. Set remaining banana half aside.

3. Mix in sugar, egg, maple syrup and vanilla.

4. In a separate bowl, whisk together flour, baking soda and salt. Then add dry ingredients into banana mixture, just until combined.

5. Pour batter into a greased 4 x 8-inch loaf pan. Lay the remaining banana half on top of batter, seeds facing up.

6. Bake for 45-50 minutes or until you can stick a toothpick in the center and it comes out clean.

7. Remove that baby from the oven and allow to cool. Once cooled, invert the loaf pan and slice to serve.

EXTRA EXTRA: For a sweeter take, you can fold 1/2 cup of chocolate chips into the batter, just before baking. A small handful of chopped walnuts is a great addition, too!

Creamsicle Cookies

Cats instinctively chase their tails, people love to chase each other, and I am 100% guilty of chasing ice cream trucks. There's something about that sweet melody that never fails to lure me in, note by note. All for one thing and one thing only: an orange creamsicle pop.

When I learned those dreamy flavors existed outside of a musical box on wheels, I went on a creamsicle rampage. You name it, I created it — creamsicle cupcakes, creamsicle cheesecake, creamsicle dessert bars, even creamsicle lollipops. It wasn't until I stumbled upon creamsicle cookies that I was truly satisfied.

These cookies are chewy, tangy and bring instant happiness to all they encounter. If you're on a quest for creamsicle, your search stops here.

Makes 10-11 Cookies.

1 3/4 cups flour

1/4 teaspoon salt

1 1/2 teaspoons baking powder

10 tablespoons unsalted butter, room temperature

1 1/4 cups sugar

2 teaspoons vanilla extract

1 large egg, room temperature

1 egg yolk, room temperature

2 tablespoons orange juice

1 tablespoon orange zest

1/2 cup confectioners' sugar

1. In a medium sized bowl, whisk flour, salt and baking powder together. Set aside.

2. In a large mixing bowl, use a stand or hand mixer to cream butter and sugar together for 2-3 minutes, until fluffy and light in color. Beat in eggs, orange juice, zest and vanilla.

3. Reduce mixer speed to low and add dry ingredients in sections. Mix until fully combined.

4. Cover bowl tightly and refrigerate for at least 1 hour.

5. Preheat the oven to 325°F when you're ready to get your bake on.

6. Use a ¼ measuring cup to scoop cookie dough, then roll into balls. Pour confectioners sugar into a small bowl. Roll each ball in sugar and transfer to a parchment lined baking sheet. Leave 3 inches in between each cookie. Repeat until batter is gone.

7. Bake for 13-15 minutes until the edges of the cookies begin to look golden. Remove from oven and let cool.

8. Try not to have a creamsicle seizure while you eat these. I can't have that on my cookie-loving conscious.

Peaches 'n Cream Panna Cotta

I grew up in Corning, New York. It's a quaint town known for glass-making and its infamous Gaffer District, but as a child I was more fascinated by the ice cream shop down the street from my house. Why? Four words, one harmonious lick: Peach and vanilla soft serve. It was one of those flavor twist combinations that was only available on occasion, which made you want it more. I remember exactly the way it tasted with the tiniest nibble of sugar cone. This panna cotta recipe is an ode to those sweet, sweet flavors.

Panna Cotta is a traditional Italian dessert. It's a beautifully chilled treat you can make ahead of time if you're hosting a party. If mercury is in retrograde and you need a sweet pick-me-up, it's equally as enjoyable when made for you and you only. If eating multiple servings of peaches and cream panna cotta is wrong, I don't want to be right. You know what I mean, Peaches & Cream.

Makes 6-8 Servings.

PANNA COTTA

2 1/2 teaspoons unflavored gelatin

1 cup peach juice

1/4 cup sugar

1 cup heavy whipping cream

1/2 cup whole milk

1 1/2 teaspoons vanilla extract

A pinch of salt

1/2 cup creme fraiche

PEACH SAUCE

2 tablespoons unsalted butter

3 ripe peaches, diced

1 tablespoon lemon juice

1/4 cup brown sugar

3 sprigs of thyme

1 tablespoon bourbon (optional)

1. In a small bowl, sprinkle gelatin over cold peach juice and let soften. Whisk lightly with a fork and let stand for 10 minutes.

2. After the gelatin has set, grab a medium saucepan and whisk sugar into the gelatin over low heat. Continuously stir for 3-5 minutes, until the sugar and gelatin have completely dissolved. Do not let it boil.

3. Stir in cream, whole milk, vanilla and salt. Cook for 1-2 minutes on low, then remove from heat. Add creme fraiche and whisk until smooth.

4. Pour mixture into ramekins and cool to room temperature. Then cover and refrigerate for at least 5 hours.

5. To prepare the sauce, begin by melting butter in a medium saucepan. Add peaches, lemon juice, brown sugar and thyme; stir over medium heat. Cook for 7-9 minutes until the peaches start to soften. If using, stir in bourbon and cook for 1 additional minute.

6. Over a small bowl, use a spatula to push the sauce through a mesh strainer. Transfer sauce to your serving vessel and cool to room temperature. Set aside until you're ready to serve.

7. Top panna cotta with peach sauce. Serve it up.

S'mores Bark

Say hello to the easiest dessert you'll ever make. It's no secret that s'mores are basically America's sweetheart when it comes to sweets. Now you can make them in the comfort of your own kitchen, no campfire required.

I love making this bark because it's highly customizable. Since you're working with melted white chocolate wafers, you can easily swirl in a little flavored extract or mix in drops of gel food coloring for a multi-colored treat. Also very important to note, I used a blowtorch to roast my marshmallows. If you don't have one, you can snag one on Amazon prime for less than $10.

Makes Enough to Share.

3 cups white chocolate melting wafers

1/8 cup milk chocolate chips, melted

1/4 cup miniature marshmallows

1 graham cracker panel, crushed

Sprinkles or extra chocolate, for garnish, optional

1. Begin by melting white chocolate in a double boiler. Fill a pot with 2 inches of water and bring to a simmer over medium heat. Place a heat-proof bowl directly over the water and fill it with white chocolate. Stir chocolate until melted. If using food coloring, remove from heat and mix in your color of choice.

2. Pour white chocolate onto a parchment-lined baking sheet. Use a spatula to smooth.

3. Place milk chocolate chips in a microwave safe bowl. Microwave the chocolate in 15-second intervals, until melted.

4. Top white chocolate base with graham crackers and marshmallows. Torch marshmallows to toast. Finish with a drizzle of melted milk chocolate.

5. Set in a cool place to let chocolate harden. You can refrigerate it to speed up the process, too. Once completely hardened, break chocolate into shards.

6. Bite it. Then have yourself s'more.

CUSTOMIZE IT: Mix a few drops of peppermint extract into melted white chocolate for a minty s'more. Finish by topping the bark with crushed oreos in place of graham crackers.

IF IT'S YOUR TURN TO HOST BRUNCH

What's one syllable, starts with a "B" and ends with the best boozy memories? BRUNCH. When I lived in Manhattan, the quest for the perfect brunch was never ending. Bottomless mimosas bubbling into champagne flutes, stacks of chocolate chip pancakes and sunshine kissing the faces of your favorite friends around the table. It's like celebrating your birthday every weekend without worrying about counting your face wrinkles.

This chapter will make you want an extra sip of those celebratory Sundays. Especially, if it's your turn to host a brunch party.

Bloody Mary Deviled Eggs

This recipe was coincidentally born on a hot weekend in June - the peak of brunch season. My friend and I were lost in a starvation-driven brainstorm about where to have brunch when we decided to make it at home. My eyes lit up like an illegal firework in the dead of summer when the words "Bloody Mary Deviled Eggs" flew out of his mouth and into the air. I was instantly determined to turn this idea into a dish that people would be proud to pass around at their own brunch gatherings.

After testing, tasting and sharing, I can honestly say these eggs taste just like our beloved bloody. When you finish preparing them, close your eyes and pop one into your mouth. Your taste buds will do the talking.

Makes 18 Servings.

12 large eggs, boiled + peeled

1/4 cup mayonnaise

1 1/2 tablespoons hot sauce (Cholula is my go-to)

2 teaspoons worcestershire

1 teaspoon tabasco sauce

1/4 cup canned Cento chopped tomatoes, drained

1 tablespoon tomato paste

1/2 teaspoon celery salt

1/4 teaspoon smoked paprika

1/2 teaspoon black pepper

1/4 teaspoon garlic powder

1 teaspoon lime juice

2-3 prosciutto slices

Garnish with prosciutto straw, dill, spicy pickle wedge, paprika, olive slice or tabasco

1. Preheat oven to 350ºF.

2. Roll prosciutto slices into tiny 1-inch "straws." Place on a lined baking sheet. Bake for 10-12 minutes, until extra crispy. Set aside.

3. Hard boil the eggs. Place eggs in the bottom of a large pot and cover them with water. Over medium heat, bring the water to a roaring boil. Once boiling, remove the pot from the heat and cover. Let sit for 10 minutes. Remove eggs from the pot and immediately transfer them to a large bowl of ice. Once cooled, peel hard boiled eggs. Cut 9 of them in half. Remove and reserve the yolks. Set hollowed egg whites aside.

4. Combine 3 whole eggs, yolks, mayonnaise, hot sauce, worcestershire, tabasco, chopped tomatoes, tomato paste, celery salt, smoked paprika, black pepper, garlic powder and lime juice into a food processor. Blend until smooth and creamy. Taste to adjust seasoning. If you prefer a spicier egg, add a pinch of cayenne pepper into the mixture.

5. Transfer mixture into a piping bag. If you're not a modern day Martha Stewart and don't own a piping bag, snag a sandwich bag and cut off the bottom corner. Pipe yolk mixture into egg whites. Garnish with prosciutto straw, small slices of pickle and sliced green olives.

6. For an interactive component, set up a DIY garnish bar for guests to build their own. Strut your brunch stuff, babe!

Everything Bagel Naan with Lox

Everything Bagels have always held a special place in my heart... and stomach. Perfectly distributed poppy and sesame seeds with hints of dried garlic and onion. And who could forget the chunky flakes of salt that instantly melt the moment they touch your tongue? Everything Bagels are exactly that - everything. They're also something I would generally never opt to make at home.

This recipe, on the other hand, is achievable, approachable and will undoubtedly satisfy your Everything Bagel cravings. Just imagine: cream cheese generously smeared across a warm naan pillow, covered with a blanket of smoked salmon adorned with capers, red onions and fresh dill. It just so happens to hit all the right flavor notes, and unlike the infamous bagel, this recipe is highly shareable. You may also have leftover "everything" seasoning for tomorrow's egg breakfast, so, you're welcome.

Makes 6-8 Servings.

NAAN

1 1/2 cups warm water

2 teaspoons sugar

2 teaspoons active dry yeast

1 1/2 teaspoon salt

3 cups flour, plus more for floured surface

2 tablespoons plain full-fat yogurt

SEASONING

1 tablespoon poppy seeds

1 tablespoon white sesame seeds

1 tablespoon black sesame seeds

1 tablespoon dried garlic flakes

2 tablespoons dried onion flakes

2 tablespoons flaky sea salt

TOPPINGS

2 cups cream cheese

1/2 cup capers

1/2 red onion, sliced thin

1 1/2 pounds smoked salmon

Fresh dill, for garnish

1. In a large bowl, combine warm water, sugar, and yeast in a bowl. Let stand for 10 minutes until foamy.

2. Add salt, flour and yogurt, then use your hands to mix until combined. Knead dough on a floured countertop, about 25 times, until the dough is smooth and passes the poke test. To test if it's kneaded to perfection, roll dough into a ball and poke it with your finger. If the indentation springs back, you're ready to move onto the next step.

3. Coat the inside of a medium bowl with olive oil, place the dough in the bowl and cover tightly. Put in a warm place to rise for 40 minutes. It will only rise slightly.

4. Drop dough back onto a floured workspace. Divide equally into six pieces and use a rolling pin to roll one eighth-inch thick pieces.

5. In a small bowl, mix all seasoning ingredients together. Sprinkle seasoning generously on both sides of dough.

6. Grill naan pieces on a grill or electric griddle; a cast iron pan works great, too. Cook for 1-2 minutes on each side.

7. Smear cream cheese on each piece of naan, top with sliced red onion, smoked salmon and capers. Garnish with fresh dill.

8. Slice and eat.

Prosecco Love Potion

I originally developed this cocktail recipe for a Channel 8 Valentine's Day segment. It was the finishing touch of a "Things to Make at Home on Valentine's Day" menu. At the time, it felt seasonally appropriate - the flawless marriage of ingredients, the undying romance associated with bubbly prosecco and the sweet, but bitter finish that sometimes comes with love. But the more I drink it, the more I realize its true purpose takes a seat at the brunch table.

Brunch foods can be on the sweeter side, which is probably why I gravitate towards herbaceous cocktails like this one. I love the depth of basil's aromatics, the peppery bite next to its strong, sweet scent. It's especially amplified when paired with muddled strawberries and dry prosecco. Even if this cocktail doesn't make you fall in love with someone else, you'll definitely love yourself more after drinking it.

Makes 6 drinks.

BASIL SIMPLE SYRUP
1/3 cup water
1/3 cup sugar
1 bunch of basil

COCKTAIL
1 bottle of dry prosecco
3/4 cup fresh strawberries, muddled
Candied ginger or strawberry slice, for garnish
Vodka, to float (optional)

1. In a small saucepan, bring water, sugar and basil to a boil. Stir until sugar is completely dissolved. Set syrup aside to cool. Remove basil when ready to serve.

2. Swirl about 2 tablespoons of muddled strawberries and 1 tablespoon of basil simple syrup into the bottom of each glass.

3. Top with prosecco. Garnish with candied ginger or a strawberry. Top with a vodka floater, for a little more oomph.

4. Sip and seal with a kiss.

Speck Wrapped Poblano Peppers

Poblano peppers are a weirdly endearing vegetable. Unlike their spicy cousin, the jalapeño, poblanos are mild in flavor and have a meaty, earthy vibe. Because they're larger in size, they also make for an excellent hand-held snack that lasts longer than two bites. It might be the gluttony talking, but when it comes to brunch, bigger is better!

You'll find this recipe to be savory and salty with a touch of smoke from the speck. If you're new to speck, it's an aged, uncooked, salted and smoked pork that you can find at your local butcher shop or grocery stores like Whole Foods. These poppers are like little wrapped gifts from the brunch gods. I know you and your crew will love them.

Makes 24 Servings.

12 poblano peppers, halved

12 ounces cream cheese

1 cup sharp cheddar cheese, grated

1/4 teaspoon white pepper

1/2 teaspoon salt

1/4 teaspoon onion powder

24 slices of speck, sliced thin

1. Preheat the oven to 400°F.

2. Line a baking sheet with aluminum foil.

3. Slice poblano peppers in half. Rinse to remove seeds and core.

4. In a medium bowl, combine cream cheese, cheddar, white pepper, salt and onion powder. Mix until fully incorporated.

5. Stuff each poblano pepper with cheese mixture. Then, wrap the peppers in speck and arrange on prepared baking sheet.

6. Bake for 25 minutes, or until the speck is crispy.

7. Serve piping hot.

NOTE: Feel free to experiment with mixing in your favorite cheese, in place of the cheddar. Brie, aged gouda or fontina would be an excellent addition. You can also add cooked ground sausage for a heartier snack.

Cannoli French Toast

In my opinion, the power of a classic Cannoli is seriously underestimated. It's not just an Italian version of the Choco Taco, it's a symphonic meeting of ingredients that can literally live together in any setting. This recipe is the perfect example.

French Toast embodies everything I believe to be French. It's sexy, alluring and isn't afraid to flaunt its flavorful personality. I wouldn't be surprised if it wore red lipstick and chain-smoked long cigarettes, either. It also happens to be an ideal pairing for the sweet, creamy filling that makes the Cannoli. Did I mention there are chocolate chips involved, too?

There are three reasons you'll want to share this recipe at your next brunch party. One, while fusing two cultures together on one plate may sound challenging, it's actually quite simple. Two, you can serve this individually plated or on one large platter – the level of sophistication in presentation is your call. Three, it's beyond beautiful and shockingly delicious. Consider this a sweet declaration that dessert belongs on the breakfast table.

Makes 8 Slices.

FRENCH TOAST

8 slices of brioche

2 tablespoons unsalted butter

3 eggs

3/4 cup milk

2 tablespoons sugar

1 teaspoon ground cinnamon

1/4 teaspoon nutmeg

1 teaspoon vanilla extract

CANNOLI CREAM

1 cup whole milk ricotta, strained

8 ounces mascarpone cheese

3/4 cup confectioners' sugar

1 1/2 tablespoons vanilla extract

1/2 cup semisweet mini chocolate chips

Confectioners' sugar + maple syrup, to garnish

1. In a large skillet, melt butter over medium heat.

2. Whisk together eggs, milk, sugar, cinnamon, nutmeg and vanilla in a shallow pie plate. Submerge bread in mixture to generously coat each piece.

3. Fry bread slices on medium heat until delightfully golden brown, 1-2 minutes per side.

4. Use a cheesecloth or mesh towel to strain the liquid from the ricotta cheese. Whisk ricotta, mascarpone, confectioners' sugar and vanilla extract together in a medium sized bowl.

5. Fold in miniature chocolate chips.

6. Layer French toast and cannoli cream. Garnish with confectioners' sugar and maple syrup.

7. Serve.

Negroni Ice Pops

I'll never forget the first time I ordered a Negroni. I was sitting with my cousin and his wife at Frankie's 457 Spuntino, a famous Italian restaurant in Brooklyn. It was positively freezing outside and pre-pasta liquor was the obvious way to warm up before our appetizers landed on the table. Upon first sip, I wasn't sure what to make of its bossy bitterness. The next sip was more complex, filling my mouth with layers of juniper and zesty citrus. By the time I reached the bottom of the glass, I had already ordered a second one. I was hooked.

If you're a boozy cocktail lover, chances are you've already sipped on this popular Italian concoction. A classic Negroni is composed of three parts: one part gin, one part vermouth rosso and one part Campari, garnished with a freshly shaved orange peel. These popsicles prolong the heavenly experience that is the Negroni, one lick at a time.

Makes 8 Popsicles.

1/2 cup water

2 ounces gin

2 ounces sweet vermouth

2 ounces campari

2 cups grapefruit juice

1/2 cup orange juice

1 orange, halved + sliced

1. Mix the liquid ingredients together in a medium bowl.

2. Pour into ice-pop molds, then drop one half of an orange slice into each mold.

3. Freeze for at least 5 hours.

4. To remove, run warm water over the mold and gently pull to release.

5. Lick it and love it.

WHAT TO EAT WHEN YOU'RE WILDLY HUNGOVER

Hangovers suck. This chapter exists to make them 100% more bearable.

Need I say more?

You Say Potato, I Say Po-Taco

Baked potatoes are a gift from the universe that should never be taken for granted. They're the obvious choice, when salted and roasted, to pair with a medium-rare New York Strip Steak, and the heart of every hash brown you've ever eaten. As if being responsible for French fries wasn't enough, they're also the key ingredient in vodka, which is pretty damn impressive. If you ask me, they work harder than every other vegetable.

Amongst my favorite potato applications, I find the Po-Taco to be most fun. It's the hybrid potato taco that you never knew you needed. This recipe serves one, but is easily doubled or tripled to feed hungry friends.

Makes 1 Serving.

1 russet potato, baked

1 teaspoon olive oil

Sea salt, for seasoning

2 tablespoons salted butter

4 ounces ground beef, seasoned with a hefty pinch of each: salt, pepper, chili powder, paprika, cumin, garlic powder + 1 tablespoon hot sauce

1/3 cup of cheddar cheese, shredded

1/4 cup tomatoes, chopped

1 tablespoon sour cream

Green onions, for garnish

NOTE: For more taco indulgence, flip to page 134 and whip up a batch of the best guacamole ever. It's a great addition!

1. Preheat oven to 375°F.

2. Scrub the potato under cold water, then pat dry. Use a fork to poke tiny steam holes throughout the spud. Then lovingly rub olive oil and sea salt on it.

3. Bake the potato directly on the middle rack of the oven for 50-60 minutes, until the skin is crispy and the interior is soft.

4. Meanwhile, add ground beef to a small skillet over medium heat. Season with salt, pepper, chili powder, paprika, cumin, garlic powder and hot sauce. Cook meat until it's browned, then drain the fat and set aside.

5. Remove potato from the oven and slice open. Use a fork to mash the inside of the potato. Top with butter, ground beef and cheese. Broil on high for 2 minutes or until cheese is melted.

6. Finish with tomato, sour cream and green onions. Add a dash of hot sauce if you're feeling extra spicy.

6. ENJOY THAT PO-TACO.

Ahi Tuna, Avocado + Cream Cheese Egg Rolls

The thing about sushi is that no matter how much you eat, you always want more of it. For me, I especially crave it when I'm hungover. When I lived in Manhattan, struggling through eight hours of work due to happy hour the night before wasn't uncommon. Unwinding over a drink (okay, fine, three drinks) is practically an unspoken requirement when you work in the hospitality industry.

I remember walking home to my shoe box sized apartment one day in the middle of a snow storm, reciting my sushi order in my head. When I finally got to my front door, my tuna avocado roll and Kani salad would be delivered and gone before I knew it. And I'd be royally distraught, aka still hungry.

It was in that moment that I decided I didn't need delivery. I just needed a do-over. A self- proclaimed experiment that would ease my sushi cravings and keep men on delivery bikes just a little warmer. Because nobody likes frostbite. These babes are crunchy, packed with fresh sushi-grade tuna and taste like happiness. Introducing the only egg roll I've ever loved. I hope you love them too.

Makes 4 Rolls.

4 wonton wrappers

8 ounces sushi-grade tuna, sliced

1 avocado, peeled + sliced

2 teaspoons red chili paste

4 ounces cream cheese

1 egg, lightly beaten

Vegetable oil, for frying

Sea salt, for seasoning

Soy sauce, for dipping

1. Step one, slice the tuna lengthwise into 2-ounce pieces. Use a brush to coat tuna with chili paste on both sides. Generously salt each piece.

2. Arrange wonton wrappers in front of you to look like diamonds. Lay two slices of avocado in the center of each wrap as a base. Top with a slice of tuna, followed by 1 ounce log of cream cheese.

3. Next, in a small bowl, use a whisk to gently beat one egg. Brush the inside of the wonton wrapper with the beaten egg. Fold the bottom point of wrapper over filling and roll once. Then fold in right and left corners, and roll to complete the egg roll. Repeat until all wrappers have been filled, brushed and rolled.

4. Heat 3-4 inches of vegetable oil in a large pot. Bring to a boil. Fry egg rolls 2 minutes per side, until crisp. You want to crisp the wrapper, but just enough so that the tuna remains rare.

5. When golden brown, transfer the egg rolls onto a paper towel to absorb remaining oil.

6. Serve with a side of soy sauce for dipping.

7. EAT YOUR SUSHI LOVING HEART OUT.

Leftovers Frittata

Don don donnnn... So, you made a few really tasty dishes this week and you're not sure what to do with all of the leftovers. If you're anything like me, you'll probably shove them in the back of your refrigerator, hoping the container magically empties and cleans itself. Still crossing my fingers for this to become a reality one day.

A better idea is this: use your leftovers to make a gorgeously fluffy frittata. This is one of those "everything but the kitchen sink" recipes, because you can really modify it however you want. The perfect frittata is like the perfect cocktail. It doesn't matter if there's three main ingredients or seven. The individual ingredients are less important than the bite that combines them all into one succulent experience.

I'm excited to share one of my favorite leftover-inspired recipes and encourage you to create your own too!

Makes 8 Servings.

4 tablespoons butter, separated

1 red onion, peeled, sliced thinly + caramelized

1 teaspoon sea salt

1 teaspoon fresh thyme, minced

8 ounces crimini mushrooms, sliced

1/4 teaspoon garlic powder

8 large eggs

1/2 cup heavy cream

1 1/2 cups fontina cheese, shredded

1 baked potato, sliced thinly

10 slices of cooked applewood bacon, roughly chopped

Salt + freshly cracked black pepper, for seasoning

Mixed greens, for garnish (optional)

1. Melt two tablespoons of butter in a skillet over low heat. Slice onions, about ¼ inch thick, and stir them into the butter. Season with sea salt.

2. Cook for 45-60 minutes, stirring occasionally, until onions deepen in color and caramelize. Once they've taken on a jammy consistency, they're ready.

3. Meanwhile, melt the remaining butter in a large skillet over high heat. Add fresh thyme and sliced crimini mushrooms and sauté for 2-3 minutes, until softened. Season with garlic powder, and a pinch of salt and pepper.

4. Preheat the oven to 400°F.

5. In a large bowl, whisk eggs and heavy cream together lightly. Fold in cheese, baked potato, cooked bacon, onions and mushrooms into the eggs.

6. Pour mixture into a greased 12-inch cast iron skillet. Bake for 15-20 minutes. When the frittata is set in the middle, remove it from the oven.

7. Serve. Akuna frittata.

Breakfast in Bread

Breakfast has this awful stigma for being reserved for mere moments after we wake up. The truth is, when you muster up the courage to ask your significant other if he wants to have breakfast for dinner, the answer is usually 'yes' accompanied by a Cheshire cat smile. Why? Because it feels like a special treat.

Breakfast in Bread is quite literally that. It's a tasty way to enjoy AM flavors, no matter where you are in your day, from a new perspective. You can easily make this recipe gluten-free, just use your favorite loaf of gluten-free bread.

Makes 2 Servings.

2 slices of sourdough bread

2 tablespoons butter

1/4 teaspoon garlic salt

4 large eggs

1 tablespoon sour cream

2 heaping teaspoons caviar

3-4 chives, cut thinly

Salt + pepper, to taste

1. Melt butter in a skillet over medium heat. Toast bread until golden on each side, about 1-2 minutes per side. Sprinkle each slice with garlic salt and set aside.

2. In a small bowl, lightly whisk eggs together. Pour eggs into a skillet over low heat.

3. Continuously whisk while the eggs begin to scramble, about 2-3 minutes. Remove from heat and whisk in sour cream until smooth. Return to heat for 30 seconds, continuing to whisk. Eggs should be semi-runny and creamy. Season with salt and pepper.

4. Plate eggs on top of toasted bread. Garnish with a dollop of caviar and freshly snipped chives.

5. Dig in immediately.

NOTE: Caviar isn't 110% necessary, but we only live once, so why not? Secondly, this is truly best enjoyed while reading The New York Times with an espresso in arms reach.

NEW YORK, MAY 5, 2019

©2019 The New York Times Company

"All the News to Print"

ded by gangs in one of
little but their tiny pa

I'd love to hear what you all think
about that. If camp began as a
kind of private language, it is now,
I think, the lingua franca of pop
culture — along with irony. I
mean, so many things are camp.
We were talking just before about
the Kardashians . . .

CHARLES What's the difference be-
tween just pop culture and camp?
I'm not quite sure. Why are the
Kardashians camp?

JAMES I don't think the Kardashians are camp at all.

ZALDY If you think of the level of
artifice of what it is to be a Kardashian — like, somehow, miracu-
lously, they all look exactly the
same now. They've all been
tempted to look like a Kardashian
that, to me, is so camp.

Doesn't camp have to
you giggle at least? Camp,
like a wife going to her
funeral wearing a Day-
 less and a big feather
d.

certain things that
ld agree on as
w disappeared
far removed
subversive.
ld still be
is there
es it have to b

I'm curious a
camp sensibili
For all of you,
you absorbed f
environments
Watching
70s vari
camp, th
of m
Evel
rol Bur
Brady
Family

ish.

whoever has en-
camp has en-
the 'S
WOW
this w
and b
on at
sensi
read
think
cult
I'm
this
on.'
it something t

work because
it just goes
working with
camp, just b
Paul, and w
Working wi
camp.
In a way,
don't really
a part of ho
my outlook
myself as ca
doing drag.

Kimchi Fried Rice

Hangovers are the worst... but are they really? Suddenly, you're allowed to snuggle on the couch without feeling like you're missing something. You get to slow down, drink a morning after Bloody Mary and maybe even put your phone on airplane mode. It's kind of like an unwelcomed pause button on the hustle and bustle of life.

What makes these days even better is when your significant other offers to cook fried rice for you. Hello, ultimate bliss. This recipe is inspired by him and the flavors of Hawaii. It's the kind of dish that will take your taste buds on a tropical vacation when you have zero energy to peel yourself away from your bed. It's also the perfect meal for a classic Netflix + Chill sesh. Sweatpants not included.

Makes 4 Servings.

1 cup Jasmine rice

1 1/2 cups water

2 tablespoons unsalted butter

6 ounces spam, thinly sliced

1 1/2 teaspoons sesame oil

1/2 medium yellow onion, chopped

1 large carrot, cubed

2 cloves garlic, roughly chopped

1/4 cup low sodium soy sauce

2 tablespoons oyster sauce

1/2 cup kimchi

1 head of baby bok choy

1 egg

Salt + pepper, to taste

1. Prepare the Jasmine rice first! Bring 1 cup of uncooked rice and 1 ½ cups of water to a boil, season water with a pinch of salt and butter. Cover the pot and reduce heat to low. Simmer for 15 minutes, then uncover and fluff with a fork. Allow the rice to cool, then refrigerate for 30 minutes to an hour. Cold rice is happy rice when it comes to fried rice.

2. While the rice is cooling down, fry spam over medium heat in a large non-stick pan until crisp. Think bacon, my friends. Remove from pan and set aside.

3. Heat sesame oil over medium heat in the same pan. Add onion, carrots and garlic, cook until tender, about 5-7 minutes.

4. Mix in chilled rice, soy sauce, oyster sauce, cooked spam and kimchi. Let the flavors harmonize for 5-7 minutes over medium heat.

5. Add bok choy and cook for 1-2 minutes until slightly wilted.

6. Meanwhile, whisk one egg lightly in a small bowl. Pour beaten egg into a small non-stick pan and cook over low heat. (I like to drop a little coconut oil into the hot pan before cooking my eggs).

7. Fry the egg in a single layer for 1-2 minutes. Use a spatula to chop into small pieces, then stir the cooked egg into the rice.

8. To serve, scoop fried rice into bowls. Add a little sriracha, if you're feeling spicy.

SALADS YOU WON'T WANT TO SHARE

There comes a time in everyone's life when all you really want is a salad. They're a fresh break in between heavy, savory meals and the notorious go-to for anyone watching their waistline.

For me, salads are a personal playground after a trip to the farmer's market. I haven't always had a solid appreciation for salads, though. When I worked in an office, my lunches literally consisted of one hard boiled egg, fresh spinach, tomatoes, sliced cheddar cheese and a tiny handful of raw almonds. Immensely boring looking back on it, but it checked my green leafy salad box for the day.

Salads don't have to be boring. In fact, I've come to know them as tiny celebrations of texture and big flavors hosted inside of one gigantic bowl. Consider this chapter your invitation to the party.

Butter Lettuce with Delicata Squash + Pomegranate Seeds

If you live in a seasonless state like I do, *em hem Florida,* it's easy to miss fall and all of its flavors. The palm trees stay green all year round, and sipping on a steamy mug of apple cider in 81 degrees feels a little wrong. Sometimes I find myself dressing for fall in hopes of encouraging the temperature to drop. Spoiler alert: it never does. Since I can't physically experience the autumnal magic, I cook it at home. This salad is fall on a plate.

Makes 4 Side Servings.

DRESSING

To make the dressing, whisk together:

3 tablespoons extra virgin olive oil

1 tablespoon balsamic vinegar

1/8 teaspoon red pepper flakes

1/4 teaspoon salt

1/8 teaspoon oregano

SALAD

1 delicata squash, sliced + roasted

2 tablespoons olive oil

1/4 teaspoon salt

1/2 teaspoon black pepper

1 head of butter lettuce, washed + leaves torn

1/4 cup sunflower seeds, toasted

1/4 cup pepita seeds toasted

1 cup pomegranate seeds

1/3 cup basil, chopped

1/2 cup ricotta salata, shaved

1. Preheat the oven to 375°F.

2. Rinse squash, then cut it in half, length-wise. Use a large spoon to scoop out seeds. Cut the squash into half-inch slices. Arrange slices in a single layer on a parchment-lined baking sheet.

3. Drizzle the squash with olive oil, then season generously with salt and pepper. Shake the sheet to coat each slice.

4. Bake for 25-30 minutes, flipping the squash halfway through the roasting process. While you're waiting, prepare the dressing.

5. When the squash is ready, remove from the oven and cool to room temperature.

6. Place lettuce, sunflower seeds, pepita seeds, pomegranate seeds, basil and squash in a large serving bowl. Toss with salad dressing until thoroughly coated.

7. Top the salad with shaved ricotta salata, salt and black pepper.

8. Serve.

Citrus Salad with Whipped Ricotta

I have a little secret. And since you're taking sweet personal time to read this, I'm going to tell you. One of the real reasons I love salads is because they're incredibly beautiful. I realize that's borderline shallow, but life feels so much better when you surround yourself with pretty, edible things. This citrus salad definitely qualifies.

Bright pops of citrus lay on a bed of honey whipped ricotta, creating a smooth symphony of acidity with a touch of sweetness. The toasted pine nuts give this fork and knife salad a rich, buttery crunch. To amp up this recipe, add one cup of greens. If sunflower shoots are in season, they add a delicate, nutty flavor into the mix. If not, the peppery bite from arugula is equally as rewarding.

Makes 4 Servings.

1 cup of ricotta cheese

3 tablespoons honey

2 oranges, peeled + sliced

2 grapefruits, peeled + sliced

1 meyer lemon, peeled + sliced

1/4 cup pine nuts, toasted

10 mint leaves, torn or kept whole

1 - 2 tablespoons olive oil

1/2 teaspoon sea salt

1/4 teaspoon black pepper

1. In a small bowl, whisk together ricotta and honey until smooth and creamy.

2. Use a brush or spatula to paint ricotta mixture onto a large serving plate.

3. Arrange orange, grapefruit and lemon slices on top of ricotta. Top with toasted pine nuts and mint leaves.

4. Finish the salad with a drizzle of olive oil, sea salt and coarse black pepper.

5. Share it, or don't. Either way, you should eat it immediately.

Endive with Watermelon, Goat Cheese + Sunflower Seed Gremolata

Watermelon is basically the Jesus Christ of all fruits. It's my go-to for granita, the obvious staple for a summer picnic and one of the most versatile flavors to work with, especially in a salad.

This recipe honors the magic of watermelon in every way I can think of. Its juicy sweetness is accentuated by the bitterness from the endive. The sunflower seed gremolata packs a citrusy, herb-forward punch that's nutty on the finish. Cool, thoughtful clumps of tart goat cheese tie a perfect white ribbon around this gift of a salad. For a more leafy take, add kale.

Makes 4 Servings.

GREMOLATA

1/8 cup olive oil

1/2 cup parsley, roughly chopped

1 garlic clove, grated

1 blood orange, zested

1 tablespoon blood orange juice

1/4 cup sunflower seeds, toasted + roughly chopped

1/4 teaspoon sea salt

SALAD

6 Belgian endive hearts, peeled + halved

2 1/2 cups of watermelon, sliced in half-inch pieces

2 ounces goat cheese, crumbled

1. In a large serving bowl, mix together olive oil, parsley, garlic, blood orange zest and juice, sunflower seeds and sea salt to make the gremolata.

2. Add watermelon and endive to the bowl and toss to coat thoroughly.

3. Finish with goat cheese and an extra sprinkle of sea salt.

4. Serve and savor.

Roasted Beet + Raspberry Salad with Savory Yogurt

First, you should know that it took everything in me not to start this paragraph with a "let's turn up the beet" pun. Although, that doesn't change the fact this salad makes me want to dance.

Roasted beets taste like the earth. Their deep, rich color is a true reflection of their dark, almost minerally flavor. Some people are turned off by this root vegetable, but this recipe promises to transform the non-believers into beet loving freaks. What I love most about it is how well the textures play together. When you're dragging a forkful of beets through white, gingery dressing, you may pick up a toasted cashew along the way. Or even better, a fresh raspberry that adds a little extra pop to your bite.

Makes 2 Servings.

3 beets, quartered + roasted

5 thyme sprigs

4 green onions, sliced lengthwise

1/4 cup of olive oil

1/8 cup cashews, toasted + crushed

1 cup greek yogurt

1 garlic clove, grated

1 teaspoon ginger, grated

1/2 cup fresh raspberries

Sea salt + black pepper, to taste

NOTE: I like to enjoy this as a side salad, but you can easily make it into a meal. Pairing it with a handful of your favorite leafy greens or a piece of grilled chicken will do the trick.

1. Preheat the oven to 375°F.

2. Scrub fresh beets under cold water until clean, then slice them into quarters.

3. On an aluminum foil lined baking sheet, arrange beets with thyme and green onions in a single layer. Drizzle with olive oil, season with salt and pepper.

4. Roast for 55-60 minutes. Remove from oven and set aside.

5. While the beets are cooking, toast cashews over medium heat in a small pan for 1-2 minutes. Once nuts become golden brown and fragrant, remove from pan and crush them into tiny pieces.

6. In a large bowl, whisk together yogurt, garlic and ginger. Taste and season with salt and pepper.

7. Spoon yogurt dressing across your serving dish. Top with beets, onions and raspberries. Garnish with toasted cashews and flaky sea salt.

8. Serve.

Prosciutto with Cantaloupe, Honeydew + Bocconcini

This recipe combines three of my favorite ingredients: prosciutto, melon and cheese. Growing up in an Italian family, antipasti frequently made an appearance on the kitchen counter before dinner was served. Cured black olives were piled high next to flawlessly rolled slices of salami. Chunks of sharp provolone stuck with confetti-topped toothpicks, marinated artichoke hearts and a dish of garlicky roasted red peppers were key staples, too. But the first thing I always reached for was a prosciutto wrapped melon ball.

While some may not classify this as a salad, it's one of my favorite ways to start a meal. It's highly shareable, addictive and fun to assemble. I mean, once you get the hang of balling the melon and cantaloupe, the rest is a breeze. Think salty notes from the prosciutto, sweetness from the fruit and a cool, mild addition from the mozzarella. Just what the Italian doctor ordered.

Makes 6 Servings.

1/2 honeydew melon, seeds removed + balled

1/2 cantaloupe, seeds removed + balled

12-15 slices of prosciutto, torn

8 ounces fresh baby mozzarella cheese balls, bocconcini or ciliegine, drained

2 tablespoons olive oil

Coarse salt + black pepper

Handful of fresh basil leaves

1. In a large serving platter or bowl, mix together melon, cantaloupe, prosciutto and Bocconcini. Drizzle with olive oil.

2. Garnish with coarse salt and black pepper.

3. Mix in a handful of fresh basil leaves for an extra pop of flavor.

Watermelon Radish Carpaccio with Kumquat + Avocado

Judging by their outward appearance, you'd never know that watermelon radishes are notorious for being a garnish. However, the second you slice one open, said mystery is immediately solved. Their loud, hot pink interior tells a vibrant story we should all be reading on repeat. So, while they're an obvious choice for a stunning finishing touch, this recipe deems them the star of the salad.

I like to think of watermelon radishes as a gateway radish. The don't have an obnoxiously spicy flavor (like their cousin the breakfast radish) and since they're so beautiful, they have a celebrity-like quality. It's my personal hope that they'll also lead you to exploring other unusual ingredients. For example, the kumquat. If you've never eaten one before, they are miniature sweet and sour oranges, bursting with citrus flavor. The best part? You can eat them whole. When they're mingling with radishes and the mellow, butteriness of an avocado it makes for an A+ party on your plate.

Makes 2 Servings.

Juice of 1 lemon

1 tablespoon olive oil

1/4 teaspoon flaky salt

1/4 black pepper

Pinch of garlic powder

2 watermelon radishes, sliced paper thin

1 avocado, peeled, seeded + sliced

1/2 cup of kumquats, sliced

2 cups of arugula

1. In a small bowl, whisk together lemon juice, olive oil, salt, pepper and garlic powder.

2. On a serving plate, arrange watermelon radish slices in a single layer. Scatter avocado and kumquat slices on top.

3. In a separate bowl, toss arugula with half of the dressing. Mound arugula in the center of the plate.

4. Drizzle remaining dressing over the entire salad.

5. ENJOY.

DATE NIGHT

It's Friday night and the work week is finally over. You walk through your front door, and the very first thing you do is dramatically collapse on the couch. It's as if you've just completed the New York City Marathon and your legs refuse to carry you one milli-step forward. Then you're supposed to muster up the energy to get up, take a second shower and groom yourself for a night out with your significant other? I DON'T THINK SO.

Date night is the best night, because once you hit your mid-twenties, it becomes acceptable to stay in. And honestly, why wouldn't you want to? Cooking at home with your person is a fun way to spend time together and the wine refills come with zero financial responsibility. This chapter is a sweet and savory ode to you and yours. I hope you love it.

Chicken Francese

There are few things in this world that are better than Chicken Francese. It's debatable, sure, but nothing revels in a lemony white wine sauce quite as perfectly as a lightly breaded piece of pan-fried chicken. I grew up on Chicken Francese, on miscellaneous school nights, during holidays and even eating it for breakfast on occasion. What can I say? Leftovers are life. It's just one of those dishes you eat and want to make, again and again.

This dish is immaculate by itself, but can be served with rice, roasted potatoes or a little bit of pasta. You can also never go wrong with a side of broccoli, sautéed with garlic and extra virgin olive oil, either.

Makes 4 Servings.

Canola oil, for frying

1 1/2 cups flour

1 teaspoon salt

1/2 teaspoon pepper

2 eggs, beaten lightly

2 pounds boneless, skinless chicken breast

5 tablespoons unsalted butter

Juice of two lemons

2/3 cup white wine

2 cups chicken broth, plus 1 tablespoon flour

2 lemons, sliced

Salt + pepper, to taste

Chopped Italian parsley, to garnish

1. In a large pan, heat 1-inch of canola oil over medium-high heat.

2. Whisk flour with salt and pepper in a small bowl. Pour seasoned flour into a large dish. Beat the eggs lightly in a large bowl. Set both aside.

3. On a cutting board, cut the chicken breasts in half, lengthwise. Use a mallet or rolling pin to pound chicken slices until they're a quarter-inch thick.

4. Dip the chicken in egg, then flour. Pressing the chicken into flour to form a thin coating on both sides. Shake each piece off before frying.

5. Fry chicken for 2-3 minutes per side or until golden. Transfer cooked chicken to a wire rack lined with paper towels to absorb the oil. Repeat until all chicken is cooked.

6. Discard the oil and use a paper towel to wipe out the frying pan. Return pan to the stove and melt butter with lemon juice and white wine over medium heat. Bring to boil and let cook for 2-3 minutes.

7. Whisk one tablespoon of flour into chicken broth, then stir mixture into the sauce. When the sauce starts to boil again, add cooked chicken and lemon slices into the pan. Simmer for 3-5 minutes.

8. Serve chicken by itself or with mushroom studded rice or pasta. Top with extra sauce and chopped parsley.

Gouda Polenta with Spring Vegetables

Preparing polenta is a lot like love. Which is one of the reasons why this recipe fits nicely into this chapter. It requires time, attention and a lot of stirring, but the meal you get in return is so worth it. I'm talking lots of warm and fuzzy feelings, friends.

This dish is hearty, vegetable-forward and can be made in under an hour. It's wonderful by itself, but also tastes great when topped with beef short rib or a nice pork shank. The vegetables can be swapped out for others in season, too. Just grab whatever looks good at your local farmer's market.

Makes 4 Servings.

POLENTA

2 cups of water

3 cups of chicken broth

1 cup yellow cornmeal

2 tablespoons butter

3/4 cup aged gouda cheese

1/2 teaspoon salt

1/4 teaspoon pepper

VEGETABLES

3 tablespoons salted butter

2 garlic cloves, crushed

1/3 cup peas

1/2 bunch asparagus, halved + ends trimmed

1 bunch broccolini, ends trimmed

1 bunch radishes, halved + greens removed

2 green onions, sliced

1/2 cup white wine

Salt + pepper, to taste

1. In a medium pot, bring water and chicken broth to a boil. Gradually whisk in cornmeal, stirring constantly to avoid clumps. Continue to whisk for 2-3 minutes, then reduce the heat to low. Season with salt and pepper.

2. Cook polenta for 45-50 minutes, stirring occasionally. Add 1/2 cup of water to thin out the polenta while cooking, if necessary.

3. Meanwhile, melt butter over medium heat in a large pan. Stir in crushed garlic and peas. Cook for 2-3 minutes, until garlic becomes fragrant and peas begin to soften.

4. Add asparagus, broccolini, radishes and green onions to the pan and season with salt and pepper.

5. Pour white wine over vegetables. Cover and cook for 5-7 minutes until vegetables are tender. Taste to adjust seasoning. Set aside.

6. Taste the polenta to check for doneness. It should be soft and creamy. When ready, remove pot from the heat; stir in 2 tablespoons of butter and gouda cheese. For a looser polenta, stir in a few tablespoons of water until it reaches your desired consistency.

7. Plate polenta in serving bowls and top with vegetables. Garnish with edible flowers for a little hint of va-va-voom.

Saltine Cracker Crusted Grouper

This recipe is the unofficial chicken nugget of the sea. Grouper is a meaty, flaky fish that shows up with grace on every plate it appears on. It's insanely good blackened, grilled, fried or baked and has a distinctively delicious flavor. It's also what I most looked forward to after my waitressing shifts in college - because it was the only time I could eat it on a scholarly budget.

This recipe is inspired by the Saltine-crusted Tripletail my grandfather used to make for my sister and I. Once upon a time, he was a Long Island fisherman who never failed to come home with armfuls of lobster and the day's fresh catch. He introduced me to Tripletail during a summer our family spent together in Melbourne Beach. It's ridiculously hard to find in stores, but grouper is a close second.

Makes 2 Servings.

1-pound grouper fillet, skinned

Pinch of coarse salt

1 large egg, whisked

1 tablespoon water

1/4 cup flour

1/4 teaspoon pepper

1/4 teaspoon paprika

1/8 teaspoon cayenne pepper

1 cup saltine crackers, finely crushed

3 tablespoons coconut oil

1. Rinse fillet under cold water. Use a paper towel to pat dry. Season lightly with coarse salt.

2. In a shallow dish, whisk the egg and water together. In a second dish, combine flour with pepper, paprika and cayenne. Lastly, place Saltine cracker crumbs on a large plate.

3. Coat fillet lightly in flour. Then dip fillet into egg mixture and dredge with Saltine cracker crumbs. Shake excess off.

4. In a cast iron or nonstick pan, warm coconut oil over medium heat. When the oil is hot, fry the fillet for 3-4 minutes per side or until golden brown. When it's ready to eat, the fish should easily flake with a fork, and temp at 145°F.

5. Serve.

Reverse-seared Steak with Asparagus

Bone-in ribeye is the king of all steaks. If you love filet mignon and want to fight over this, you know where to find me. The reason why I put ribeye on a steak pedestal is because of how buttery and flavorful it is. It's a thick cut from the cow that's rich with white marbling (also known as fat, but hey, marbling sounds better), making it the perfect candidate for a reverse-sear.

I prefer to reverse-sear my steak because I'm the woman who routinely sends steaks back to the kitchen if they're a touch over medium-rare. Using this technique, it's pretty difficult to fuck up the temperature. It'll always be cooked perfectly. The most important rule when reverse-searing: keep your eyes on the steak temperature while it's in the oven.

Makes 2 Servings.

STEAK

1-2 pound bone-in ribeye steak

Coarse salt + black pepper

2 tablespoons unsalted butter

3 thyme sprigs

1 rosemary sprig

2 garlic cloves, smashed

ASPARAGUS

1 asparagus bunch, ends removed

1 tablespoon olive oil

1/8 cup parmesan, finely grated

Garnish with zest of 1/2 lemon

Sea salt + pepper, to taste

For the Steak

1. Preheat the oven to 250°F.
2. Season the (room temperature) steak with coarse salt and cracked black pepper. Don't be afraid to generously season!
3. Place steak on an aluminum-lined baking sheet. For a medium-rare steak, cook until the center reaches 115°F. This can take 25 - 45 minutes depending on how thick it is. The key is to watch it closely.
4. When the steak reaches 115°F, remove it from the oven.
5. In a cast iron skillet, melt butter over high heat. Add thyme, rosemary and garlic.
6. Sear the steak for 45 seconds to 1 minute, on each side. Brown it up, baby! When it reaches 130°F remove it from the skillet.
7. Let rest for 5 minutes, then slice and serve.

For the Asparagus

1. Fill half of a large pot with water. Bring water to a boil over high heat.
2. Rinse and prepare the asparagus. Cut off and discard the inedible "woody" ends. No one likes those.
3. Blanch the asparagus in boiling water for 3-4 minutes. Then strain.
4. Toss with olive oil, parmesan and lemon zest. Season with salt and pepper. Serve.

Cacio e Almost Pepe

Say hello to the most lavish adult mac n' cheese you'll ever meet. The first thing you should know is that "Cacio e Pepe" means cheese and pepper in Italian. The second, is that it's traditionally served with Spaghetti. Today we're breaking all the rules and treating ourselves to a sexy bowl of Bucatini.

Bucatini is basically the hollow sister of spaghetti, which means more swimming room for sauce.... Remember that long styrofoam pool toy with a hole in it? IT'S CALLED A NOODLE. It should really be called bucatini.

This recipe is perfect for any day, at any time. But I especially crave it when I'm in the mood for a serious bowl of comfort. It's a 20-minute date night dish that says, "you could eat me at a restaurant, but well done, for making me at home." So, it comes with a side of instant gratification. We all need a little more of that, don't we?

Makes 2 Servings.

8 ounces bucatini

1-2 tablespoons black pepper, freshly cracked + toasted

1 tablespoon unsalted butter

1/2 cup salted pasta water

1 1/2 cups pecorino romano cheese, plus more for garnish

1/2 cup grana padano cheese

Sea salt + pepper, to garnish

1. Bring a large pot of salted water to a boil over high heat. Add bucatini to the water and cook for 8-10 minutes, until al dente. Drain and reserve 1 cup of pasta water.

2. Meanwhile, toast freshly cracked pepper in a large skillet over medium heat. Cook for 2-3 minutes until the pepper starts to jump around in the pan. I like to call it the pepper dance.

3. Reduce the heat to low, then add butter and 1/2 cup of the pasta water to the skillet. Whisk together. Turn the heat off.

4. Transfer al dente pasta to skillet and use tongs to stir in cheese, continuously tossing to coat each strand generously. Add more of the reserved pasta water for a looser sauce vibe.

5. Plate and garnish with additional pecorino, pepper and a light dusting of salt.

Vanilla Mascarpone Cupcakes with Lavender Frosting

Call me on my bullshit if I'm totally out of bounds here.... But aren't cupcakes just a sexier rendition of muffins accessorized with a fancy mound of frosting? Because I personally feel like there's no clear distinction between the two. Well, I previously felt that way, until I whipped up a batch of these vanilla mascarpone cupcakes.

If you're looking for a moist and pillow-soft kind of cupcake, look no further. Mascarpone gives these miniature cakes an angelic, cloudlike texture. I'm calling it in advance that you'll be tempted to put mascarpone in everything you bake from this moment forward. Don't say I didn't warn you.

Makes 12 Cupcakes.

CUPCAKES

1 1/2 cups flour

1 teaspoon baking powder

1 teaspoon baking soda

1/2 teaspoon salt

1/2 cup unsalted butter, room temperature

1 cup granulated sugar

2 large eggs, room temperature

1 tablespoon madagascar vanilla extract

1/2 cup mascarpone

LAVENDER FROSTING

8 ounces cream cheese, room temperature

4 tablespoons unsalted butter, room temperature

2 3/4 cups confectioners' sugar

2 teaspoons vanilla extract

1-2 drops lavender essential oil

2-3 tablespoons milk

1. Preheat oven to 350°F. Line a 12-count muffin tin with cupcake liners.

2. In a large bowl, whisk together flour, baking powder, baking soda and salt.

3. In the bowl of a stand mixer fitted with the paddle attachment, beat butter and sugar until light and fluffy.

4. Beat in eggs one at a time, then vanilla. Add in the mascarpone and mix until fully combined.

5. Gradually add dry ingredients to wet ingredients and mix on low speed, just until incorporated.

6. Scoop batter into cupcake liners. Bake for 16-18 minutes, or until you can insert a knife in the center and pull it out cleanly.

7. Remove from the oven and let cool. Transfer cupcakes to a wire rack to cool completely.

8. For the frosting, use an electric mixer to beat together cream cheese and butter on high, until fluffy. Add in vanilla and confectioners' sugar gradually, beating on low for 2 minutes. Mix in lavender essential oil and milk.

9. Frost the cupcakes and eat!

Cookies n' Cream Zeppole

When I was in the crazy season of recipe testing for this book, I spent a lot of time sourcing recipes from my family. This zeppole recipe actually hails straight from Italy, from my great- great-aunt. Even though I've never met her, it's nice to know she'll always be remembered through this book.

Zeppole are an Italian dough that's formed into a ball and deep fried. They're similar to a doughnut or a churro, but in my opinion, reign supreme. This recipe makes a cakey pastry that gets dressed in a coating of crushed Oreos. If you'd rather try the classic preparation, skip the cookies and dust them with confectioners' sugar. Either way, these sweets must be served hot and pair wonderfully with vanilla ice cream!

Makes 24 Servings.

1 cup warm milk

2 teaspoons active dry yeast

2 tablespoons sugar

1 teaspoon vanilla

1/2 teaspoon salt

2 1/4 cups flour

3 eggs, lightly beaten

1/4 cup unsalted butter, melted

6-8 Oreos, crushed finely

1/3 cup confectioners' sugar

1. Pour milk into a small bowl, then add the yeast, sugar, vanilla and salt. Let stand until creamy, about 2 minutes. Then stir to dissolve the yeast.

2. In a large mixing bowl combine flour, eggs and butter with the yeast mixture. Stir with a wooden spoon until a nice sticky dough forms. This should take around 8-10 minutes.

3. Cover the bowl tightly with plastic wrap and let the dough rise in a warm place for 1 1/2 hours.

4. Pour 3-4 inches of vegetable oil in a deep heavy bottomed pot. Heat the oil to 370°F (use a frying or candy thermometer to double check temperature).

5. Use two tablespoons to shape the dough, then drop into the hot oil. The goal is to make perfectly round pieces.

6. Fry 4 zeppole at a time, making sure not to crowd the pot. Cook until golden brown and puffy, turning with a slotted spoon to fry evenly on all sides.

7. Remove cooked zeppole from the oil. Transfer to a drying rack lined with paper towels to absorb the oil.

8. Immediately shake the zeppole with crushed oreos and confectioners' sugar in a brown paper bag.

9. Serve piping hot.

WHEN ALL YOU WANT IS PASTA

Pasta is like the friend who always calls you back. The one who answers your texts within five minutes of receiving them. The person who lets you cry on their shoulder when someone else eats your leftovers. I've also been told it's really satisfying after a hard workout, but I haven't had one of those since the 8th grade gym class mile, so I'll take your word for it.

As an Italian, it's basically my job to have an indisputable affinity for pasta. This chapter might be your favorite, if you do too.

Pasta with Shiitakes & Creamy Cajun Sauce

Cajun sauce has always been on my 'like list,' but up until now I had convinced myself it was reserved for eating out. Never did I ever think I'd be making it at home or writing about it in a cookbook.

If you're a sauce enthusiast, I encourage you to add this recipe to your to-do list. It's creamy without feeling heavy and has layers of faraway flavors in every bite. The best part about this recipe is how easy it is to modify. If you want to add chicken, go for it. Entertaining vegetarian guests? No problem. Just substitute butter for olive oil, and swap the cream and chicken stock for equal parts of vegetable broth. See what I mean? Easy, delicious and 100% transformable.

Makes 4 Servings.

16 ounces rigatoni

2 tablespoons unsalted butter

2 tablespoons olive oil

2 garlic cloves, chopped

1 shallot, sliced

4 cups shiitake mushrooms, sliced

1/2 teaspoon red chili pepper flakes

1 teaspoon chili powder

1/2 teaspoon cumin

1/2 teaspoon smoked paprika

1/4 teaspoon cayenne pepper

2 teaspoons sea salt

2 cups cherry tomatoes

1 cup chicken stock

1/2 cup heavy whipping cream

1/2 cup parmesan cheese, to garnish

1. Fill a large pot halfway with salted water and bring to a boil over medium heat. Add pasta and cook for 8-10 minutes, per the box's al dente preparation. Once ready, strain and set aside.

2. In a large pan, melt butter and olive oil over medium heat. Add garlic and shallot. Sauté for 1-2 minutes until fragrant.

3. Stir in mushrooms, red chili pepper flakes, chili powder, cumin, smoked paprika, cayenne pepper and salt. Cook for 3-5 minutes, and allow mushrooms to soften.

4. Add cherry tomatoes to the pan. Cook for 5 minutes until tomatoes begin to blister. Listen for the pop when the skin splits!

5. Next, deglaze the pan with chicken stock, using a wooden spoon to scrape any brown bits off the bottom of the pan. Stir cream into the sauce. Simmer for 2-3 minutes on low.

6. Toss pasta in sauce and scoop into serving bowls. Garnish with grated parmesan cheese.

7. Devour immediately.

Zucchini   Lemon Pasta with Pecorino

I'm not carb-loading, you're carb-loading! I mean, if you're cooking through this chapter, perhaps we both are.

This recipe is my go-to when I'm craving a light pasta dish. There's just something so uplifting about lemon, cheese and zucchini together on a plate. Zucchini is in its peak season from May to August, making summer the perfect time to stock up. If you can't get your hands on it for this recipe, a yellow squash or Patty Pan squash are solid substitutes. As is, this dish is vegetarian-friendly! Add oven-baked chicken breast for a heavier dish.

Makes 2 Servings.

8 ounces of your favorite pasta

3 tablespoons butter

2 tablespoons olive oil

1/4 teaspoon red pepper flakes

3 garlic cloves

2 zucchini, grated

1/2 teaspoon salt, to taste

Zest of 1 lemon (about 2 tablespoons)

2 tablespoons lemon juice

1/3 cup reserved pasta water

1/2 cup parmesan reggiano, plus more for garnish

1. Fill a large pot halfway with salted water and bring to a boil over medium heat. Add pasta and cook in boiling water for 8-10 minutes. Once ready, reserve 1/3 cup of pasta water, strain and set aside.

2. In a separate large pan, melt butter and olive oil over medium heat. Add red pepper flakes and garlic. Sauté for 1-2 minutes until fragrant.

3. Stir in grated zucchini, salt, lemon juice and zest, plus reserved pasta water. Cook for 2-3 minutes. Stirring frequently.

4. Mix in cooked pasta and cheese. Toss to coat.

5. Scoop into serving bowls. Garnish with more grated Parmesan cheese. Because cheese makes everything better.

When I was a miniature Melissa,

I used to sit on the kitchen counter and watch my parents make Sunday Sauce. Being eye-to-eye with the process was very important. Everything was done with such care and I was determined to soak up every detail.

The forming of the meatballs was especially fascinating to me. My mom and dad gently rolling them back and forth between their seasoned hands. Little bits of meat occasionally getting stuck to their fingers, refusing to surrender their pre-sauce pride. And when the last ball sunk into that glorious red pot, I knew it was almost time. **Ricotta time.**

After what seemed like a lifetime worth of minutes, the meatballs were cooked. The sauce would remain on low heat for hours after this point, but I never waited. Because being a tiny rebel is an area all Aquarians excel in.

Moments after I knew the sauce was semi-ready, I b-lined it to the fridge in search of our residential giant tub of ricotta. Then I'd grab a small dish, plop a scoop of ricotta in the middle and drown it in sauce until it disappeared. Spooning it into my mouth before letting it cool was also my thing. It was worth every mouth burn.

While I don't recommend downing the Sunday Sauce as it's piping hot, I do suggest tasting as it cooks and adjusting the seasoning as you see fit. I always find myself adding an extra pinch of salt!

You can beef up this Sunday Sauce recipe by adding a slab of pork spare ribs into your sauce. If you opt to do so, season one pound of ribs with salt and pepper, then brown them in a large cast-iron or enameled pan over medium heat. It will add about 10 minutes onto your sauce journey, but will result in heaps of melt-in-your-mouth pieces of pork. Just drop the browned ribs into the sauce after step number 5.

FLIP FOR THE GOOD STUFF ⟶

Sunday Sauce

Welcome to my weekly sauce tradition. I hope this recipe finds a permanant spot at your dinner table, too.

Makes 8 Servings.

SAUCE

1/4 cup olive oil

1 white onion, chopped

2 1/2 teaspoons sea salt

1 teaspoon red pepper flakes

1/4 teaspoon fresh thyme leaves

1/2 teaspoon oregano

8 garlic cloves, crushed

1 cup red wine, I like to use chianti

3 28-ounce cans of San Marzano whole peeled tomatoes

1 28-ounce can of tomato sauce

1 cup water

Pecorino romano, ricotta + fresh basil, to garnish

MEATBALLS

1 pound grass fed ground beef (80% lean/20% fat)

1 pound ground pork

1 1/2 teaspoons parsley

1/2 teaspoon onion powder

1 teaspoon salt

1 teaspoon black pepper

2 cups parmesan cheese, grated

2 eggs

1 1/2 cups bread crumbs

1/2 cup water

Olive oil, for frying

1. In a large pot, heat olive oil over medium heat. Add onion, salt, red pepper flakes, thyme and oregano. Cook onions down until soft, making sure to stir frequently, about 7-9 minutes.

2. Stir in garlic and simmer until fragrant, about 2 minutes. Then pour in wine.

3. Use a blender to purée whole peeled tomatoes. Add blended tomatoes and sauce into the pot. Bring to a boil then reduce to low heat.

4. For the meatballs, use your hands to mix all ingredients together in a large bowl. Before rolling the meatballs, dip your fingers in warm water, then roll into two to three-inch balls.

5. In a frying pan, heat 1-2 inches of olive oil over medium heat. When hot, brown meatballs in batches. Immediately after meatballs are browned, drop them into the sauce. You do not want to cook them all the way through. Before discarding the frying oil, stir 1 tablespoon into the sauce.

6. Reduce the sauce heat to a simmer and cook for 4-5 hours. Halfway through cooking, add 1 cup of water to the sauce. Taste to adjust seasoning.

7. Serve with your favorite pasta, ricotta cheese, fresh basil leaves and shaved pecorino romano cheese.

8. MANGIA.

Garlicky Vodka Sauce with Shrimp

Penne with vodka sauce is a dish I relentlessly order at restaurants and consistently make at home. I think I love it so much because of how my dad used to make it. Then again, I love everything he does because that man is a modern day saint. In all sincerity, my childhood friends still rave about his legendary vodka sauce.

Depending on where you are geographically, vodka sauce has a handful of different preparations. Some people use vodka in their recipe while others don't, bacon is sometimes substituted for pancetta, and then there's the restaurants that label vodka sauce as "pink sauce." My point is, not all vodka sauces are created equally, but you're going to loooove this recipe. This garlicky sauce is smooth, tangy and so, so, so silky. The addition of shrimp gives it a little more substance, and is especially nice when you're cooking for a crew with big appetites.

Makes 4 Servings.

1 pound penne pasta

1 tablespoon olive oil

1 pound shrimp, cleaned + deveined

3 tablespoons butter

4 ounces diced pancetta

1 shallot, minced

4 garlic cloves, sliced

1/2 teaspoon red pepper flakes

1 teaspoon sea salt

1 tablespoon tomato paste

1/4 cup vodka

1 28-ounce can of San Marzano whole peeled tomatoes

1/2 cup heavy cream

1/2 cup grated parmesan

Pecorino romano, chunky finishing salt, torn pieces of fresh basil, for garnish

1. In a large frying pan, heat olive oil over medium heat. Arrange shrimp in a single layer, sprinkle with salt and pepper. Cook 1 minute per side, until shrimp turns pink. Remove from heat and set aside.

2. Prepare pasta al dente, per box directions. Fill a large pot halfway with salted water, bring to a boil and cook penne for 8-10 minutes. Strain and set aside.

3. In a large pot, melt butter over medium heat. Cook diced pancetta for 4-5 minutes, until crisped. Remove it from the pan and set aside. Add shallot, garlic, red pepper flakes and sea salt; cook for 1 minute.

4. Stir in tomato paste and cook until it begins to deepen in color. Pour in vodka and use a wooden spoon to loosen up any bits on the bottom of the bot.

5. Use a blender to purée whole peeled tomatoes. Add blended tomatoes and crisped pancetta into the pot. Bring to a boil, then reduce to low heat. Let simmer for 10 minutes.

6. Remove from heat, then stir in heavy cream and parmesan until the sauce lightens to a smooth, singular color. Add the cooked shrimp into the sauce and simmer on low for an additional 2 minutes.

7. Toss vodka sauce with penne. Garnish with pecorino romano, chunky finishing salt and torn pieces of fresh basil. Serve!

Pasta e Fagioli

There are three things you should never live without: Peace, Love and Pasta e Fagioli.

In raw translation that's actually four things because Pasta e Fagioli means "pasta and beans" in Italian. On the contrary, it's also the name of a classic Italian soup that found its way onto my childhood kitchen table - rain, snow or shine. I have fond memories of my parents showing me how to chop the onions and garlic to kick off the recipe. Their aroma dancing in the air as soon as they landed in a hot bath of olive oil. I danced too, because I knew what was coming. This soup is rustic comfort food with layers and layers of flavor. That's all you need to know.

Makes 4 Servings.

2 tablespoons good olive oil

3 garlic cloves, roughly chopped

1/4 teaspoon red pepper flakes

3 slices of prosciutto, roughly chopped

1/2 medium onion, roughly chopped

1 celery stalk, cubed

2 carrots, chopped

1/2 teaspoon sea salt

1/2 teaspoon rosemary, chopped

2 thyme sprigs

1 15-ounce can of cannellini beans, drained

32 ounces chicken broth

1 bay leaf

2 cups cooked ditalini

Salt and pepper, to taste

Garnish with finely grated pecorino

1. In a large Dutch oven or heavy-bottomed pot, warm olive oil over medium heat. Add garlic, red pepper flakes and prosciutto, cook for 1-2 minutes or until you begin to smell that beautiful scent that reminds me of home, aka garlic.

2. Stir in onion, celery, carrot and salt; cook for 5-7 minutes until translucent. Add rosemary and thyme. Cook for an additional 1-2 minutes.

3. Stir 3/4 can of cannellini beans into the pot. Use a fork to mash the remaining beans inside the can, then stir the bean paste into the pot. This will help thicken the soup. Cook for 3-5 minutes.

4. Add chicken broth and bay leaf, cover and simmer on low for 25 minutes.

5. Meanwhile, prepare pasta in a separate pot. Cook according to box directions until al dente. Drain and set aside.

6. When ready to serve the soup, remove bay leaf and thyme sprigs. Stir in pasta and taste to adjust seasoning.

7. Ladle into bowls and top with finely grated pecorino cheese. ENJOY!

Bolognese for Everyone

Bolognese is another classic Italian stunner. It's the perfect option for the meat lover in your life and will satisfy your friend who's a self-proclaimed sauce connoisseur. Originating from the city of Bologna, it's a sauce that's typically served with a pappardelle or tagliatelle. I'm not that old school, so I say, make it with whatever pasta you're in the mood for.

There's one exceptionally important ingredient in this recipe and it's not the organic ground beef. It's a spice that I've fallen head over feels in love with and a little goes a long way. FRESH NUTMEG. If you don't have fresh nutmeg in your spice cabinet, this is the one ingredient I'll beg you to run to the grocery store for. Trust me, it makes a delightful difference in the depth of flavor. Skip the cream for a dairy-free alternative.

Makes 4 Servings.

12 ounces pasta, literally any shape

1 pound organic ground beef

3 tablespoons olive oil

2 celery stalks, cubed

2 carrots, cubed

1/2 white onion, chopped

3 garlic cloves, roughly chopped

1/4 teaspoon red pepper flakes

2 tablespoons tomato paste

1 cup dry white wine

1 28-ounce can of whole peeled san marzano tomatoes

1 rosemary sprig

1 oregano sprig

1/2 nutmeg kernel, grated

3/4 cup heavy cream

Sea salt + cracked black pepper

Ricotta salata, pecorino cheese or parmesan reggiano, for garnish

1. In a large pan, cook ground beef over medium heat until browned, 5-7 minutes. Season with salt and pepper. Remove from pan.

2. Use a paper towel to soak up any remaining oil in the pan. Then add olive oil over medium heat.

3. Stir in celery, carrots, onion, garlic and red pepper flakes. Sauté for 7-9 minutes until vegetables begin to soften. Then add in tomato paste, cook for 1-2 minutes.

4. Deglaze the pan with white wine, using a wooden spoon to scrape up any burnt bits.

5. Use your hands to crush the San Marzano tomatoes into small chunks. Then add tomatoes, rosemary and oregano into the pot. Bring to a boil, then reduce heat to a simmer and cook for 15-20 minutes.

6. Meanwhile, fill a large pot halfway with salted water and bring to a boil. Add pasta and cook for 8-10 minutes. Strain and set aside.

7. Finally, stir shaved nutmeg and heavy cream into the sauce. Add the ground beef. Cook for an additional 3-5 minutes on low heat.

8. Toss pasta in sauce and serve. Garnish with ricotta salata, pecorino cheese or parmesan reggiano.

DINNER PARTY UPGRADES

I wrote this chapter because even though I spend a lot of time in the kitchen, for some reason I always have trouble deciding what to cook for friends. When I'm planning a meal, all of a sudden the kitchen becomes this big scary place full of possibilities. And I'm left standing there with tons of anxiety. If you can relate, this chapter is here to save your ass in moments of need. Happy entertaining, friends!

Tuna Crudo with
White Truffle Oil + Manchego

One of my favorite snacks in the world is this tuna crudo. It's a big statement for such a little bite, but when you try it, you'll know exactly what I mean. I first locked taste buds with the inspiration behind this dish when I was in college. In fact, tuna crudo was my forever go-to after Thursday night happy hour. While most of my friends ran back to their dorm rooms for a notorious cup of soggy ramen noodles, to be enjoyed bunkside, I was giving my palette a secondary education... in food.

If you have a special place in your heart for sashimi, this recipe is going to make you a very happy human.

Makes 4 Servings.

8 ounces sushi-grade yellowfin tuna

2 tablespoons ponzu sauce, separated

1/2 tablespoon white truffle oil

1/4 cup pine nuts

Shaved manchego cheese + pinch of Maldon sea salt, for garnish

1. Lightly brush the middle of 4 appetizer plates with 1 tablespoon of ponzu sauce. Season the base with a sprinkle of sea salt.

2. Next, use a fillet or boning knife to slice tuna into half-inch thick pieces. An extra sharp, non-serrated knife is important to create flawless slices!

3. Lay tuna slices over seasoned base ingredients. Drizzle white truffle oil over fish, garnishing each slice with a thick shaving of Manchego cheese, 2-3 pine nuts and sea salt flakes.

4. Serve immediately with a side of ponzu or soy sauce.

Radishes with Lemony, Goat Cheese Butter

In my past life at Neuman's Kitchen, Chef Stacy Pearl taught me how to make butter. It's literally one of the easiest party tricks in the world, yet the response you get to, "I made this butter" is wildly impressive, every damn time. When you add goat cheese into said butter, the feedback is even better.

I love serving radishes with homemade butter as a pre-dinner snack. They look beautiful on a plate of hors d'oeuvres or work nicely on their own. I encourage you to experiment with infusing your favorite spices into the butter, too!

Makes Snacks for 2-3.

1 radish bunch, rinsed well + tops removed

2 cups heavy cream, chilled

1/4 teaspoon rosemary, minced

1/2 teaspoon lemon zest

1/2 teaspoon salt

2 1/2 tablespoons goat cheese

1. In a stand mixer fitted with the whisk attachment, whip 2 cups of heavy cream on medium speed until medium peaks form, about 3 minutes.

2. Increase the speed to high and whip until the solids separate from the milk. Make sure you're rocking an apron because things are about to get wet. Whip for about 8 minutes or until you hear sloshing in the bottom of the bowl.

3. Use your hands to mold the butter into a ball and squeeze out remaining liquid.

4. Transfer the ball to a strainer and rinse under cold water, squeezing, until the water runs clear.

5. Knead in rosemary, lemon zest, salt and goat cheese until combined.

6. Pat the butter dry with a paper towel, then smear across whole or halved radishes.

7. Garnish with more lemon zest, rosemary and salt, if desired. Wrap the extra butter in plastic and refrigerate.

Mango Mint Granita + Elderflower Whipped Cream

Mangoes are the Jennifer Lawrence of fruit. They're luxurious, sweet and pretty damn perfect without a stitch of makeup. Cutting and peeling a mango, however, can be an intimidating game. Although this creamy fruit is fabulous in its natural state, there's something magical about eating it by the icy spoonful.

Granita is originally from Sicily, but today you'll see it on menus all over the world. It's a dairy-free treat composed of fruit, sugar and water, most commonly enjoyed during hot summer months. I make this recipe whenever the craving strikes. Because I love you, I'm also giving you a second option for a watermelon batch.

Makes 4 Servings.

MANGO GRANITA

1 cup water

1 fresh mint sprig

1/4 cup sugar

Pinch of salt

3 ripe mangoes, peeled + diced

WHIPPED CREAM

1 cup heavy whipping cream, cold

1/4 cup confectioners' sugar

1 teaspoon vanilla extract

3 tablespoons elderflower liqueur

TRY THIS: For watermelon granita, blend together 4 cups cubed watermelon, 1/8 cup lime juice, 3 tablespoons confectioners' sugar + a pinch of salt. Then follow steps 3-5.

1. In a small pot, bring water and mint sprig to a boil over medium heat. Add sugar. Stir until dissolved, then remove from heat. Remove mint leaves. This is your simple syrup.

2. In a blender, combine syrup and mango. Pulse until mixture becomes smooth. Pour mixture into a shallow pan. I like to use a 9-inch pie dish.

3. Freeze for about 45 minutes, then rake with a fork to break up any ice crystals that form around the edges of the pan. Repeat this step every 30 minutes, for 2 hours. Then your granita is ready! If you don't want to serve right away, at this step you can cover it tightly and reserve it for the next day. I don't recommend making it more than one day in advance.

4. For the whipped cream, use a standing or hand mixer to beat heavy cream, confectioners' sugar, vanilla and elderflower liqueur, until soft peaks begin to form, about 3-4 minutes. You're looking for a fluffy cloud here.

5. Serve granita in individual dessert bowls, top with whipped cream.

Grilled Chicken Skewers with Charred Poblano Sauce

Is there anything more entertaining than listening to music and threading chicken chunks onto skewers with your friends? Just kidding. But you know you want to.

These skewers are juicy, flavorful and virtually fool-proof. If you don't have a grill, or it's the middle of winter, you can bake them at 450°F for 12-15 minutes. Just lay them on an aluminum-lined baking sheet and let the oven do the rest. You'll find the charred poblano sauce to be a creamy, welcomed addition. This dish is great on it's own, but you can serve it with a side of mushroom studded rice or stuffed baked potatoes. Whatever your people are craving, you know?

Makes 4 Servings.

CHICKEN

2 pounds chicken breasts, cubed into

2-inch pieces

1 tablespoon olive oil

1/4 cup of lime juice

3 cloves garlic, grated

1/4 teaspoon onion powder

2 teaspoons salt

1/4 teaspoon ancho chile powder

1/2 teaspoon black pepper

2 tablespoons wild honey

POBLANO SAUCE

2 roasted poblano peppers

1/2 cup plain whole fat yogurt

3 tablespoons olive oil

1/2 teaspoon salt

1/2 teaspoon white pepper

Squeeze of lime

1. In a large bowl, whisk together olive oil, lime juice, garlic, onion powder, salt, ancho chile, black pepper and honey. Add diced chicken and toss to coat thoroughly. Let marinate for 1 hour.

2. Using wooden or metal skewers, thread the chicken pieces. Repeat until chicken is gone.

3. Grill chicken skewers for 10-15 minutes, rotating occasionally to brown evenly. Remove from grill when the chicken juices run clear and set skewers aside.

4. For the sauce, blister poblano peppers on a grill or stove top element, using metal tongs to rotate and char the peppers evenly on each side.

5. When ready, remove pepper cores and seeds. Combine roasted peppers, yogurt, olive oil, salt, white pepper and lime juice in the blender. Purée until smooth.

6. Serve skewers with a side of poblano sauce!

SERVING TIP: Elevate this dish by threading 2 pieces of cooked chicken onto a fancy toothpick; repeat until all chicken is used. Then place a bowl of charred poblano sauce in the center of a circular platter and arrange skewers around it. These are great as a passed hors d'oeuvre or a family-style main course.

Braised Short Rib Ravioli with Sage + Brown Butter Sauce

Everything tastes better with short rib. Who can deny this buttery, salty, melt in your mouth meat of meats? It makes you work long and hard before being rewarded with its touted flavors, but it is always worth the wait. In fact, I may go as far to say that the only thing better than braised short rib is short rib ravioli. Luckily for you, this recipe will teach you how to make both from scratch. All you need is patience, a little bit of courage if you're a first-time pasta maker, and the right tools.

I like to serve this dish with a light brown butter sauce and a touch of sage. If you're yearning for a heavier pairing like Vodka sauce or Alfredo, click those ruby red foodie heels and make it happen. I support you!

Makes 4 Servings.

SHORT RIB

2 tablespoons canola oil

3 pounds short rib

1 head of garlic, halved

1 medium yellow onion, chopped

2 medium carrots, peeled + chopped

2 celery stalks, chopped

2 tablespoons tomato paste

2 1/2 cups of dry red wine, I prefer chianti

10 thyme sprigs

1 bay leaf

2 1/2 cups beef stock

SCRATCH PASTA

2 cups all-purpose flour

2 eggs, room temperature

1 egg yolk, room temperature

2 tablespoons water

1/8 teaspoon salt

1 egg + 1 tablespoon water for egg wash

RAVIOLI FILLING

3/4 cup short rib, room temperature + shredded

1 1/2 cup ricotta

1/8 teaspoon garlic powder

1/2 cup grana padano cheese

Salt and pepper, to taste

BROWN BUTTER SAUCE

6 tablespoons unsalted butter

10-12 sage leaves, whole

1/4 cup beef stock

1/4 cup parmesan, grated

P.S.: For your vegetarian guests, you can make the ravioli without short rib. Just skip the meat and 1.5x the filling recipe!

This recipe also makes enough short rib + sauce for leftovers. I recommend eating it over a cheesy polenta or mashed potatoes. Remove the herbs + blend the braising liquid for a silky sauce.

We're going to separate this recipe into three parts. The first involves braising the short rib. The second will focus on the pasta dough and ravioli preparation. Lastly, we'll make a sinfully easy brown butter sauce.

Part 1: Braised Short Rib

1. Preheat the oven to 350°F.

2. In a large Dutch oven, warm canola oil over high heat. Season short ribs generously with salt and pepper. Sear for 2-3 minutes per side, until golden brown on all sides. Remove from pot and set aside.

3. Add onion, carrot and celery to the pot. Cook on medium-high heat until vegetables begin to soften, about 10 minutes, then stir in tomato paste. Continue to cook for an additional 3-5 minutes.

4. Deglaze pan with red wine and add short ribs back to the pot. Bring ingredients to a boil, then lower heat to a simmer. Use a wooden spoon to scrape those crispy bits off the bottom of the pot. Stir in thyme, bay leaf and stock. Transfer to oven.

5. Cook for 2 1/2 - 3 hours, until short rib meat is tender. Remove short ribs from the sauce. Let cool and use a fork to shred.

Part 2: Pasta + Ravioli Preparation

1. Start by sprinkling a layer of flour on your countertop. Create a mound with the flour, then use your fingers to create a well in the middle. Crack eggs into the center. Add salt and water to the eggs. Then use a fork to scramble eggs, keeping them in the center of the flour mound.

2. Use your hands to gradually combine flour into wet ingredients. Once the dough starts to come together, knead until you've formed a ball. Knead for 8-10 minutes. The consistency should be smooth and elastic. When you push into the dough and it expands back towards you in response, it's ready to rest.

3. Drizzle olive oil onto the dough ball. Wrap ball tightly with plastic wrap and set aside for 30 minutes. It's time to let that baby rest. Sing it a lullaby if you feel inclined.

4. While the dough is sleeping, it's time to prepare the filling. Mix together the short rib, ricotta, garlic powder, cheese, salt and pepper in a medium bowl. Set aside.

5. After the dough has rested, cut ball into two sections. Use a pasta machine to roll out each section of dough. Run the dough through the roller several times, starting with the largest setting, then gradually transitioning down; until the pasta dough is one-eighth inch thick. You can also roll out the pasta dough with a rolling pin.

6. To assemble the ravioli, lay one pasta sheet down on a floured surface. Brush sheet with egg wash.

7. Drop one tablespoon of filling on the dough, about 2 inches apart. Cover with a second sheet of pasta, pressing gently around each filling mound to remove any air pockets. Use a circular cookie cutter to cut each ravioli. Press firmly around the edges of each piece to seal.

8. Bring a large pot of salted water to a boil. Carefully drop 4-5 ravioli in the water at a time, cook for 3-4 minutes. Strain ravioli and set aside. Repeat until all ravioli are cooked.

Part 3: Sauce

1. In a medium saucepan, melt butter over medium heat. Add sage leaves. Cook until the sage leaves begin to curl and butter begins to brown, about 5 minutes. Remove leaves and lay them on a paper towel. Whisk beef stock into brown butter. Stir in Parmesan cheese.

2. Transfer ravioli to brown butter sauce; coat gracefully. Divide amongst plates of your choice. Garnish with more grated parmesan cheese, fried sage leaves and sea salt. Serve.

Pear + Rosemary Cupcakes with Vanilla Frosting

When I bite into these cupcakes, they have a special way of biting back. A love bite, if you will. Fragrant notes of pear followed by hints of rosemary and cinnamon, wear the crown in this recipe. The cake itself is soft and fluffy. The use of cake flour in this recipe helps achieve a beautiful crumb that's moist on the inside with a gentle crunch on the exterior. The lightly salted burst of vanilla cream makes for a sweet finish.

Makes 21 Cupcakes.

CUPCAKES

2 1/3 cups cake flour, plus 1 tablespoon

1 teaspoon baking powder

1 teaspoon baking soda

1/2 teaspoon cinnamon

1/4 teaspoon salt

1 cup unsalted butter, room temperature

1 1/2 cups superfine sugar

2 eggs, room temperature

1 1/2 teaspoons vanilla extract

1/2 teaspoon grated ginger

2 pears, diced

1 1/4 teaspoons fresh rosemary, finely minced

VANILLA BUTTERCREAM

1 1/4 cups unsalted butter, softened

1 tablespoon vanilla extract

3 1/2 cups confectioners' sugar

3 tablespoons heavy cream

Fleur de Sel, for garnish

1. Preheat oven to 350°F.

2. In a medium bowl, whisk together flour, baking powder, baking soda, cinnamon and salt. Set aside.

3. In a separate mixing bowl, use a hand mixer to cream together butter and sugar. Once the mixture is light and fluffy, add the eggs, vanilla and freshly grated ginger.

4. Next, gradually add dry ingredients, scraping down sides of bowl to ensure all ingredients are thoroughly combined.

5. Use a paper towel to gently "dry" off the diced pear. Then toss the pears with one tablespoon of flour. Fold the pear and rosemary into the mixture.

6. Line muffin tins with your favorite cupcake liners, depending on the occasion. Fill each halfway with the batter.

7. Bake for 18-22 minutes, or until you can pull a clean toothpick out of the center of the cake. Remove cupcakes from oven and set aside to cool.

8. For the buttercream, use a mixer to beat the butter until light and airy, about 3 minutes. Mix in vanilla and sugar until incorporated, then add cream. Continue to beat the buttercream until it's silky and sultry.

9. Frost each cupcake. Garnish with Fleur de sel.

Black Cherry + Peach Clafoutis

When I think of clafoutis, I think of Julia Child. I think of all the hours she spent in the kitchen, experimenting with recipes and feeding them to her husband. The look on his face being a silent exclamation that she had perfected the task at hand. For some reason, I imagine it to be an incredibly special moment. It's my hope that this recipe creates a special moment for you, too.

Clafoutis is a French dessert that eats like a custard but bakes like a cake. It can truly be made with any fruit, but is traditionally served with cherries. I love making this for friends because it's super easy and quick to prepare. Best served warm with a generous dusting of confectioners' sugar.

Makes 6 Servings.

CLAFOUTIS

1 saturn peach, sliced

2 cups cherries, pitted

2 tablespoons unsalted butter, melted

1 tablespoon vanilla extract

3 eggs

1/2 cup heavy cream

3/4 cup milk

1/2 cup flour

1/4 cup sugar

1/4 teaspoon salt

Pinch of cinnamon

Confectioners' sugar, for dusting

FOR THE RAMEKINS

1/8 cup granulated sugar

2 tablespoons unsalted butter

1. Preheat the oven to 350°F.

2. Prepare 6 ramekins by buttering the inside of each one. Followed by a coating of sugar.

3. Arrange cherries and peach slices in each ramekin.

4. In a large bowl, whisk together butter, vanilla, eggs, cream and milk. Then gradually whisk in flour, sugar, salt and cinnamon until mixture is smooth.

5. Pour batter into prepared ramekins. Bake for 25-30 minutes.

6. Channel your inner Julia and serve warm with a dusting of confectioners' sugar.

NOT YOUR AVERAGE TACO TUESDAY

If you've never indulged in "taco night" at home, I'm truly sorry. They're one of the best, easiest things to whip up and no matter what, they never disappoint. Until they're gone, that is.

This chapter is your new guide to Taco Tuesday in the comfort of your own kitchen, including my number one recipe for homemade guacamole. Now, shake up a margarita and let's do this thing.

Lamb Meatball Lettuce Cups with Pistachio Chimichurri

So, you might be thinking, "Well, this is untraditional for Taco Tuesday." And, it is. We can't always stuff our faces with ground beef and salsa soaked tortilla chips, although I'll never not advocate for that. These lamb meatballs are lightly fried to lock in moisture and topped with Greek-inspired flavors. Think lamb meets feta with freshly chopped tomatoes, garnished with a bright parsley pistachio herb sauce. Welcome to my version of a healthier Taco Tuesday.

Makes 4 Servings.

LAMB MEATBALLS
1 pound ground lamb
1 egg
2 garlic cloves, grated
1 teaspoon thyme, roughly chopped
2 teaspoons parsley, minced
1/2 cup panko
1/2 cup pecorino romano
1/8 teaspoon red pepper flakes
1/4 teaspoon salt
Canola oil, for frying

PISTACHIO CHIMICHURRI
1/2 cup fresh basil leaves
1 cup parsley, packed
2 garlic cloves
1/4 cup roasted pistachios, shelled
1/4 teaspoon red pepper flakes
1 teaspoon fresh oregano
2 tablespoons red wine vinegar
1/2 cup olive oil
1/2 teaspoon sea salt

LETTUCE CUPS
1 head of romaine lettuce
2 roma tomatoes, diced
1/2 cup feta, crumbled

1. Use your hands to mix meatball ingredients together in a large bowl. Dip your fingers into a bowl of hot water, then roll meat into 1-inch balls.

2. In a large skillet, heat a half-inch of canola oil over medium heat. Cook meatballs in batches until golden brown on all sides, about 6-7 minutes. When cooked, place meatballs on a rack lined with paper towels to absorb extra oil.

3. For the sauce, combine basil, parsley, garlic, pistachios, red pepper flakes, oregano, red wine vinegar, olive oil and sea salt in a blender. Purée until smooth.

4. Serve meatballs in lettuce leaves. Top with chimichurri, tomatoes and crumbled feta.

Sunny Side Up Breakfast Tacos

Make no mistake, just because the word "breakfast" is in the title of this recipe doesn't mean they're reserved for the morning. I actually love eating these tacos for lunch and dinner. Let's be honest, who has time to make tacos before work? I'm lucky if I have enough time to make a smoothie.

This recipe is my North Star when I'm craving quick and easy tacos. It's also a one pan meal, meaning that there won't be more than 5 minutes of clean-up. The egg yolk helps create a silky bite, where a condiment or salsa would otherwise be. And who doesn't love a little pickled onions and tomatoes in their tacos?! The acid helps cut through the richness from the yolk, while adding a little something special to the overall experience.

Makes 4 Servings.

TACOS

4 eggs

1 tablespoon unsalted butter

Salt + pepper, to taste

1/2 cup cherry tomatoes, halved

1 avocado, sliced into wedges

Flour or corn tortillas, warmed

Queso fresco, for garnish

Hot sauce, for garnish

1 lime, squeezed for garnish

PICKLED RED ONION

1 red onion, sliced thinly

1/2 cup apple cider vinegar

1/4 cup water

1 tablespoon honey

1 teaspoon salt

1. For pickled red onions, combine onions, apple cider vinegar, water, honey and salt in a mason jar (or any jar with a lid). Shake to combine. Set aside for 15 minutes to get your quick pickle on.

2. In a large nonstick skillet, melt butter over medium heat. Crack eggs into the skillet and fry until the whites of the eggs are set, but the yolk is still runny. Remove from skillet and transfer each egg to their own tortilla. Season with salt and pepper.

3. Top each taco with pickled onions, tomatoes, avocado, queso fresco and a squeeze of lime.

4. Finish with a dash of Cholula if you're feeling wild.

Extra pickled onions can be stored in the fridge for up to two weeks. #powermove

Chicken, Hoisin   Cucumber Tacos

I have a confession to make. I never order chicken tacos from restaurants. It's not that I don't love chicken. Personally, I think it's one hell of a bird. It's that I'm perpetually scared of chicken that's drier than the Sahara desert. *It's thee worst.* And somehow, it always happens to me when I'm out on the taco town.

This recipe takes you through a fool-proof poaching method that only leads to a moist and delicious bite. The chicken is simmered in sesame oil and broth, then lathered with Hoisin sauce before landing on a warm tortilla. You know, the way chicken tacos should be.

Makes 4 Servings.

1 1/2 pounds skinless chicken breast, poached + shredded

1 teaspoon salt

1/2 teaspoon pepper

1/4 teaspoon garlic powder

1/2 teaspoon ginger, grated

2 teaspoons sesame oil

1 1/2 cups chicken broth

1/4 cup hoisin sauce, plus more if you want saucier chicken

1 large cucumber, peeled + diced

4 scallions, sliced

Sour cream, for garnish

Corn or flour tortillas, warmed

1. Season chicken with salt, pepper, garlic powder and ginger. Make sure to rub the spices on both sides of the chicken generously.

2. In a large skillet, heat sesame oil over medium heat. Add chicken to skillet and cook for 2-3 minutes per side.

3. Pour in chicken broth. Cover and cook for an additional 15-20 minutes or until the internal temperature of the chicken reaches 165°F.

4. Use a fork to shred the chicken. Then mix the chicken with hoisin sauce, tossing with tongs until it's completely coated. Let it sit in the skillet until you're ready to assemble the taco.

5. Place individual servings of chicken in the center of each warm tortilla. Top sliced cucumbers, scallions and a dollop of sour cream.

6. Treat yourself to that taco.

IPA Battered Cod Tacos with Coconut Cream Slaw

If I'm going to eat fish tacos, they're going to be fried. While I'll never hate on grilled or blackened fish tacos, there's something substantially more pleasing about the crispiness that comes with an IPA battered cod taco.

This recipe is exactly what I think of when I hear the words "beer battered." Dare I say that it reminds me of traditional London fish and chips with a tropical flare. The coconut cream slaw adds a nice, fresh crunch and little bit of sweetness. Don't neglect your tortillas either, whether you're using corn or flour, you should 110% warm them before assembling.

Makes 4 Servings.

SLAW

3 cups green cabbage, shredded

1/2 cup red cabbage, shredded

1/2 cup carrots, shredded

1/4 cup coconut cream

2 tablespoons olive oil

1/2 teaspoon salt

1/4 teaspoon pepper

1 tablespoon lime juice

Zest of 1/2 lime

FISH

1 pound cod, sliced into pieces

1 1/2 cups flour

1 1/3 cups IPA beer

1/4 teaspoon paprika

1/4 teaspoon onion powder

1 teaspoon salt

1/2 teaspoon ancho chili pepper

Vegetable oil, for frying

Corn tortillas, warmed

PICKLED RED ONION

1 red onion, sliced thinly

1/2 cup apple cider vinegar

1/4 cup water

1 tablespoon honey

1 teaspoon salt

1. In a large bowl, combine green cabbage, red cabbage and carrots. In a separate bowl, whisk together coconut cream, olive oil, salt, pepper, lime juice and lime zest. Set both aside. Don't toss the slaw until you're ready to serve!

2. For pickled red onions, combine onions, apple cider vinegar, water, honey and salt in a mason jar (or any jar with a lid). Shake to combine. Let sit for 15 minutes.

3. In a large heavy-bottomed pot, heat 3-4 inches of vegetable oil over high heat until it reaches 375°F.

4. While the oil is getting hot, whisk flour, beer, paprika, onion powder, salt and ancho chili pepper together in a large bowl. Sprinkle coarse salt over the fish slices, then dip into the batter until fully coated.

5. Fry 4-5 pieces at a time. Remove fish from the oil when it's golden brown and crisp. Transfer to a paper towel to absorb remaining oil.

6. Assemble the tacos in tortillas, filled with fish, dressed slaw and pickled onions.

7. EAT IT UP.

Wild Mushroom Tacos with Blue Cheese

Whenever I eat a vegetarian taco, I generally think to myself, "Why didn't I order Cochinita Pibil?!" Maybe it's the lack of body you feel in your hand as you lift it off the plate, or maybe deep down, I'm just a salty carnivore. Either way, something always feels like it's missing. This recipe is my solution to that problem.

By making mushrooms the star, you'll get a gratifying, meaty vibe from these tacos. This recipe is wonderful with portobello mushrooms, an assortment of wild mushrooms or tried and true baby bellas. Double or triple it if you're cooking for a crew.

Makes 2-3 Servings.

1/4 cup butter

3 garlic cloves, minced

1/2 shallot

2 thyme sprigs

2 pounds wild mushrooms, sliced or quartered

1 teaspoon red wine vinegar

1 teaspoon salt

1/2 teaspoon pepper

1/2 cup of blue cheese crumbles

2 avocados, peeled, pitted + sliced

Corn or flour tortillas, warmed

1. In a large skillet, melt butter over medium high heat. Add minced garlic, shallot and thyme sprigs. Cook for 2-3 minutes.

2. Stir in mushrooms, red wine vinegar and salt and pepper. Sauté until the mushrooms soften and begin to brown.

3. Fill your favorite taco shells with mushrooms. Top with blue cheese and avocado.

4. Serve.

The Best Guacamole Ever

Let me start by saying, guacamole doesn't require an occasion.

It's an admirable addition on top of scrambled eggs with a little side of salsa. Just one smear across a turkey sandwich brings your meal from an 8 to a solid 10. I've been known to make avocado toast on top of sweet potato halves too, but that's a whole new level of infatuation. Regardless of how you enjoy it, one thing will always ring true. Guacamole and tortilla chips are a TACO TUESDAY NECESSITY.

Makes 4 Servings.

4 Haas avocados, seeded + smashed

2 tablespoons lime juice

1/2 teaspoon garlic powder

1/4 teaspoon sea salt

2 roma tomatoes, diced

1 tablespoon hot sauce

2 tablespoons cilantro, chopped

1/2 medium red onion, minced

Salt and pepper, to taste

1. Have you ever seen the "Peel the Avocado" YouTube video? The first thing you need to do is look that up, watch it, laugh and then admire your avocados. If avocados had fingers, that woman would put a ring on it.

2. Halve each avocado, remove the seed and use a spoon to scoop the meat into a bowl.

3. Add lime juice, garlic powder and salt to your avocado, and mash to your desired consistency. Some people love a really smooth guacamole, I prefer happy chunks of avocado scattered throughout mine.

4. Next, stir in the tomato, hot sauce, cilantro and onion. Taste and season with salt and pepper.

5. Finally, grab your favorite tortilla chips and dip your way into the best guacamole ever.

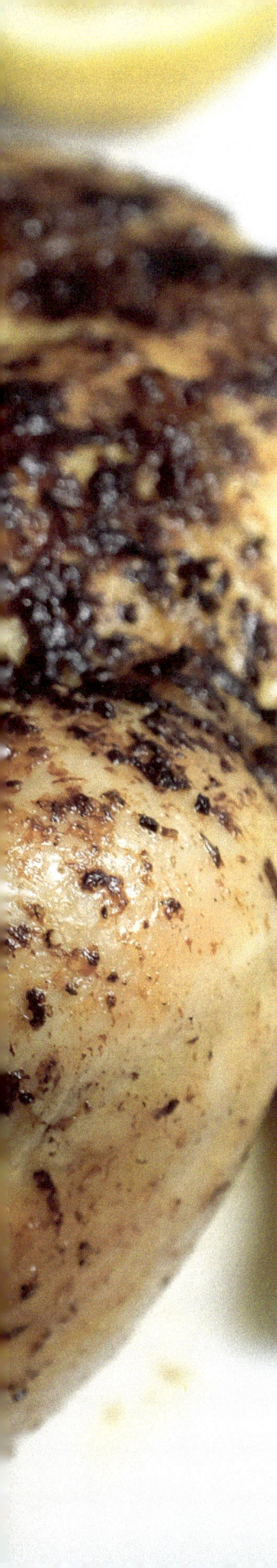

ONE PAN WONDERS

Welcome to my menagerie of all things savory and simple. This chapter is for the cook who digs an easy clean up, but craves a touch of adventure in the kitchen. Most of these dishes feel like dinner, but serve as an excellent next day lunch, too. You'll find they work splendidly for entertaining family and friends, or a low key night in with your significant other. Hello, one pan bliss.

He Loves Me Not Butternut Squash Soup

Butternut squash is one of those ingredients that's associated with a specific place and time. Hi, Fall, I'm looking at you. This soup makes me want to eat it all year round. I try my hardest to make that a reality by freezing the leftover soup, as it keeps for two to three months. Something tells me you won't have a single drop to spare, though.

I added a little touch of Greek yogurt to this recipe to help smooth and round out the soup. For a dairy-free version, skip the yogurt and add coconut cream instead. Both make for a velvety spoonful of your new favorite soup.

Makes 4 Servings.

ROASTED BUTTERNUT SQUASH

2 tablespoons olive oil

1 butternut squash, peeled, seeded + cubed

1 head of garlic, halved

2 carrots, halved

1/2 large white onion, quartered

1 teaspoon sea salt

1/2 teaspoon pepper

5 sprigs of fresh thyme

THE SOUP

2 tablespoons butter

2 tablespoons olive oil

1 Pink Lady apple, diced

1/4 teaspoon of red pepper flakes

1/4 teaspoon onion powder

1/8 teaspoon cinnamon

1 teaspoon sea salt

5 cups chicken stock

1/4 cup greek whole milk yogurt

1. Preheat oven to 400°F.

2. Arrange butternut squash, garlic halves, carrots and onions in a single layer on an aluminum lined baking sheet. Drizzle 2 tablespoons of olive oil over the vegetables. Season with salt, pepper and scattered thyme sprigs. Bake for 35-40 minutes.

3. In a large heavy-bottomed pan, melt butter and olive oil over medium heat. Add apple, red pepper flakes, onion powder, cinnamon and salt. Cook for 3-5 minutes until soft.

4. Remove thyme from roasted vegetables and peel roasted garlic. Add vegetables, roasted garlic and chicken stock into the pot. Cook for 10 minutes on medium heat, or until the soup begins to boil.

5. Reduce heat and stir in yogurt. Use an immersion blender to blend the soup. You want a velvety, creamy consistency. Taste to adjust seasoning.

6. Pour into serving bowls and garnish with your go-to hot sauce or butter fried sage.

Whole Tarragon Chicken with Fingerling Potatoes

I'm not one to shy away from a one-pan meal... Or a delicious roasted chicken. This recipe checks both boxes. It's one of those wonderful meals you can throw in the oven after work and completely forget about until it's time to eat. You could even watch an entire episode of Sex & the City with a glass of red wine while you wait.

Aside from the amazingly tender, tarragon scented chicken, one thing to look forward to is the potatoes. They'll be roasting in a bath of lemony juices, catching the aftermath of the chicken fat melting into the roasting pan. This recipe is obviously meant to be eaten while it's piping hot, but don't sleep on your leftovers. Chilled chicken is an ideal candidate for a next day chicken salad.

Makes 4 Servings.

1 (4-5) pound chicken

1/2 cup white wine

5 tablespoons unsalted butter, melted

2 tablespoons tarragon, chopped

Juice of 1 lemon + the lemon itself (about 2 tablespoons)

Coarse salt + black pepper

1 head of garlic, halved

5 sprigs tarragon

1 1/2 pounds fingerling potatoes

1/8 cup olive oil

2 teaspoons garlic powder

4-5 sprigs, thyme

1. Preheat the oven to 400°F.

2. Rinse chicken under cool water, then dry with a paper towel. Transfer to a roasting pan.

3. In a small bowl, whisk together white wine, melted butter, tarragon and lemon juice. Massage the mixture all over the chicken. Rub remaining butter underneath the skin.

4. Season the inside and outside of the chicken generously with salt and pepper. Then stuff the chicken cavity with the lemon rind, garlic and tarragon sprigs.

5. In a large bowl, toss fingerling potatoes with olive oil, garlic powder and thyme. Arrange potatoes around the chicken on the roasting pan.

6. Roast for 1 hour and 10 minutes (this can vary depending on the weight of your chicken), using a large spoon to baste the chicken as it cooks. This will help crisp the skin!

7. Broil for an additional 3-5 minutes for an extra golden bird. Remove from the oven when the internal temperature reaches 165°F. Let rest for 5-10 minutes before slicing.

8. Serve!

Harissa Roasted Yellowtail Snapper with Patty Pan Squash

Cooking a whole fish at home can be... a bit scary. The entire idea of slicing through the skin of something while it's literally watching you from a pair of dead eyes is something you'll have to work through. It's not the kind of trauma that requires therapy though, so please don't send me your doctor bill. Just kidding.

I think you'll find this recipe to be really approachable, rewarding and delicious. The harissa adds smoky and spicy layers of flavor, with citrus that keeps the bite bright. The fish and patty pan squash are roasted together on one sheet pan, making for a ridiculously easy clean up, too.

Makes 2 Servings.

2 whole yellowtail snapper, scaled + gutted

1 lemon, sliced

1 lime, sliced

1 orange, sliced

6 sprigs of thyme

3-4 tablespoons olive oil

4 tablespoons harissa

5 cups patty pan squash, halved + sliced

1 shallot, halved

Coarse sea salt + black pepper

1. Preheat the oven to 450°F. Line a large baking sheet with aluminum foil and coat it lightly with non-stick spray.

2. Rinse the inside and outside of the fish under cool water. Pat dry with a paper towel. Then use a sharp knife to make diagonal score lines on the fish, cutting just below the skin.

3. Stuff the fish with lemon, lime and orange slices, and finish with thyme sprigs.

4. Whisk 2 tablespoons of olive oil and harissa together in a small bowl. Brush mixture on both sides of each fish. Season the fish generously with salt and pepper, then place on baking sheet.

5. In a separate bowl, toss together patty pan squash, 1-2 tablespoons of olive oil, salt, pepper and shallot. Arrange squash in a single layer around the fish.

6. Roast for 15 - 20 minutes, flipping the squash halfway through the cooking time. Remove from the oven once the fish has reached an internal temperature of 145°F.

7. Serve!

Parchment Salmon with Walnut Parsley Pesto

If you're hunting for a healthy savory dish that's easy and packed with flavor, you're going to dig this recipe. By steaming the salmon in an airtight parchment pocket, you'll get a similar result to poaching it. Tender, tasty and luxurious. When the fish is ready to eat you'll get to unwrap it like a gift, which might be one of my favorite parts about this method. You'll be greeted by an ultra moist piece of fish, infused with citrus flavors and topped with an herbaceous pesto.

Makes 4 Servings.

4 (4-6 ounce pieces) salmon

2 mandarin oranges, sliced

6 sprigs of fresh dill

2 cups parsley

2 garlic cloves

1/8 teaspoon black pepper

1/2 teaspoon salt

1/4 cup olive oil

1/4 cup walnuts, toasted + crushed

Flaky salt, to garnish

1. Preheat the oven to 400°F.

2. Cut out 4 perfect parchment squares. Arrange parchment side-by-side on a baking sheet. Place 2-3 orange slices and dill in the middle of each sheet, top with salmon. Season salmon with a sprinkle of salt and pepper.

3. In a blender, combine parsley, garlic, pepper, salt, olive oil and walnuts. Blend for 30 seconds or until smooth.

4. Spoon 3/4 of the pesto on top of each salmon fillet. Fold parchment paper several times over the salmon to create an airtight pocket.

5. Bake for 10-12 minutes, depending on your preferred cook temp. My vote is always for medium rare salmon, which is 125°F.

6. Remove from oven and transfer salmon to serving plate. Garnish with remaining pesto and flaky sea salt.

7. Seerrrrve.

Chicken Thighs in a Buttery, Marsala Cream Sauce

Chicken thighs tend to be a highly misunderstood part of the bird. I too, was formerly partaking in the "breast is best" movement, until my brother-in-law fought to defend their decadent honor. For some reason, I originally thought that because thighs were cheaper than chicken breasts they were somehow inferior. But I'm here to tell you, that is not the case, my friends. Full disclosure: my sister still hates them.

I can't believe I missed out on so much time with this part of the chicken. While it's one of the most fatty pieces, what that really means is the meat will never be dry and the skin will always be prime for browning. Speaking of brown, it's also home to the most tender, dark meat of the chicken we all know and love. This recipe takes chicken thighs to a new, creamy level with a mushroom-infused marsala sauce. Eat it as is, or serve it over your favorite rice or pasta.

Makes 4 Servings.

5 tablespoons unsalted butter

4-5 chicken thighs

Salt + pepper, for seasoning

8 cloves of garlic, crushed

8 ounces baby bella mushrooms, washed + sliced

5 sprigs of fresh thyme

1/2 teaspoon red chili pepper

1 teaspoon sea salt

1 cup of marsala

2 cups of chicken stock

2 tablespoons cornstarch + 1 tablespoon water

1/2 cup heavy cream

Salt + pepper, to taste

1. Melt butter over medium-high heat in a heavy bottomed pan.

2. Season chicken with salt and pepper. Add chicken thighs to butter and sauté until crispy on both sides, about 4-5 minutes per side. Remove chicken from pan and set aside.

3. Add garlic, mushrooms, thyme, red pepper flakes and salt into the butter. Sauté for 4-5 minutes until the mushrooms begin to brown.

4. Deglaze pan with marsala, using a wooden spoon to loosen up the crispy bits. Then stir in chicken stock. Bring to a boil.

5. In a small cup, whisk 2 tablespoons of corn-starch with 1 tablespoon water. Whisk mixture into the sauce to thicken it.

6. Reduce heat to low. Add chicken back to the pan and cook for an additional 3-4 minutes on medium heat.

7. Finish by stirring in cream. Cook for 1 additional minute.

8. Serve over rice or pasta.

FANCY, YET SIMPLE SNACKS

Do you ever feel like being boujee but have zero interest in putting any effort into it? Well, this chapter will help you live as luxuriously as possible without being Beyoncé. Introducing my favorite high class snacks on an any-class budget.

Prosciutto Wrapped Figs with Honey

During my time in Manhattan, I religiously walked three blocks down Chrystie Street to Whole Foods, on a mission for freshly sliced prosciutto and Tiger Figs (when they were in season). They were the only two items I exclusively made a grocery trip for, in the middle of the work day. Despite the occasional battle with a gigantic line of hungry humans holding boxes of food from the hot bar, I always escaped unscathed.

As I'm sure you've already noticed, prosciutto is one of my fridge and life staples. I eat it by itself, fry it up for soups, make tiny rose shapes with it and have a fondness for wrapping it around fresh figs. The two are practically made for eachother.

Makes 4 Servings.

10-12 pieces of prosciutto, sliced thin

12 tiger figs

Wildflower honey, to drizzle

Flaky sea salt, to garnish

1. Wrap one prosciutto slice around each fig. You can tear prosciutto slices in half for smaller figs.

2. Drizzle figs with honey and finish with a pinch of sea salt.

3. Bite into them ferociously.

Sprout Studded Chicken Salad

Yes, cleaning and cooking a chicken can be time consuming. So, you'll find that this recipe calls for my favorite store bought time-saver, the rotisserie chicken. If you'd rather roast your own, flip to page 140 and cook your way through my recipe for Whole Roasted Tarragon Chicken.

This chicken salad is the ideal mixture of sweet, salty and spicy. Pops of whole grain mustard add texture to each bite, next to sweetness from the honey. You can totally eat this chicken salad on its own with a fork, or build it into the best picnic sandwich ever. Directions for both applications are below.

Makes 4 Servings.

CHICKEN SALAD

1 small rotisserie chicken, shredded

1/4 cup olive oil

1/4 cup red wine vinegar

2 1/2 teaspoons whole grain mustard

1 tablespoon honey

1 teaspoon salt

1/2 teaspoon black pepper

1/2 teaspoon fresh rosemary, minced

1/2 cup sliced green onions

GARLIC AIOLI

Whisk together...

¼ cup mayo

1 teaspoon lemon juice

1 garlic clove, grated

Salt + pepper, to taste

FOR SERVING

Cucumber, sliced thin

Tomato, sliced

Avocado, sliced

Microgreens + sprouts, for garnish

Whole grain bread

1. In a medium bowl, whisk together olive oil, red wine vinegar, mustard, honey, salt, pepper and rosemary.

2. Mix in shredded chicken and sliced green onions.

3. Eat the chicken salad by itself or enjoy it as a sandwich. If you're making a sandwich, smear garlic aioli on the inside of whole grain bread slices, then layer chicken salad, cucumber, tomato, avocado and microgreens.

Mustard Roasted Brussels Sprouts

Really nicely roasted brussels sprouts embody the true meaning of a fancy, simple snack. I prepare and roast them in a cast iron pan, aka my literal sidekick in the kitchen. It's one of the only pieces of kitchen gear that gets better as you use it, as a form of true appreciation for filling it with delicious food, over and over again.

For extra crispy brussels sprout leaves, the key is to put them in the oven while it's pre-heating. If you're serving this dish to a room full of vegetarian friends, skip the pancetta.

Makes 4 Side Servings.

2 tablespoons butter

1 1/2 pounds brussels sprouts, stems removed + halved

2 cloves garlic, smashed

4 ounces pancetta, diced

1 tablespoon maple syrup

2 teaspoons dijon mustard

1/2 teaspoon salt

Freshly cracked black pepper

1. Preheat oven to 450°F.

2. In a large cast iron skillet, melt butter over high heat. Add brussels sprouts, garlic, pancetta, maple syrup, dijon, salt and pepper. Stir to coat ingredients. Cook for 1-2 minutes.

3. While the oven is preheating, transfer the skillet into the oven.

4. When the temperature reaches 450°F, bake for 25-30 minutes or until the brussels leaves begin to crisp.

5. Eat them by yourself as a fancy snack, throw them in a taco or devour them with your favorite protein.

Not Your Mama's Pasta Salad

When I was growing up, cold macaroni salad has always been a huge part of my family's summer repertoire. We used to douse it in mayonnaise, pack it in picnic baskets and arrive at neighborhood BBQ's with a gigantic bowl in tow. This recipe is my version of a new kind of pasta salad.

Instead of using traditional heaps of mayo, this salad is tossed with greek yogurt-based dressing and chunks of salty feta cheese. I recommend eating it warm, but if you can't shake your 1990's ways, it tastes just as lovely after spending an hour in the refrigerator.

Makes 4 Servings.

12 ounces pasta of your choice

1 cup greek yogurt

2 1/2 tablespoons red wine vinegar

1/4 cup olive oil

3 large garlic cloves, grated

2 1/2 teaspoons sea salt

1 1/2 teaspoons black pepper

1 teaspoon chervil (or French Parsley)

2 teaspoons thyme

2 1/2 cups cherry tomatoes, halved

1 1/2 cups snap peas, roughly chopped

1 1/2 cups feta, crumbled

1. In a medium pot, boil salted water for the pasta. Cook pasta until al dente, per the box instructions. Strain and set aside.

2. In a large bowl, whisk together greek yogurt, red wine vinegar and olive oil. Whisk in grated garlic, salt, pepper, chervil and thyme.

3. Fold in pasta, tomatoes, snap peas and feta. Toss to thoroughly coat. Taste to adjust seasoning.

4. Serve warm!

Cheese + Charcuterie

Cheese and charcuterie are the epitome of an adult playground. Moldy cheeses with bold attitudes and sweet dispositions. Cured meats from every crevice across the globe. Accoutrements to hold the hands of rustic flavors and make them shine just a little bit brighter. This is modern day heaven, people. There are a million and seventeen combinations to experiment with when you're talking cheese and charcuterie. The key to a successful plate is variety in texture, appearance and flavor. You wouldn't want to wear a purple cotton shirt with purple cotton pants and purple tennis shoes, would you? No, because that's boring... and really strange, actually. If you're wearing all purple right now in this moment please consult the nearest Nordstrom stylist, immediately.

To give you an idea of how much I love this pairing, my boyfriend designed and built a table we could eat, cut and share cheese, charcuterie and all of its gloriousness on. We assemble beautiful cheese and charcuterie displays directly the table, often, and in a more civilized way than eating directly off of a table sounds. If you just got the sudden urge to buy a new kitchen accessory, google BUILT to score your very own feasting table.

This "recipe" walks you through my favorite cheeses, meats and accoutrements and how to mix and match them. First, select four cheeses that have different levels of softness, ripeness and age. Then, pick four items from the meat and accoutrements categories to finish your board! Your board should have 12 items, total.

CHEESE	MEATS	ACCOUTREMENTS
Dorothea, potato chip infused goat gouda	Prosciutto	Honey comb
Délice de Bourgogne	Duck rillette	Quince
3-Month aged manchego	Genoa salami	Crusty Italian bread
Tickler cheddar	Pâté	Caper berries
Blue cheese, like Stilton	Coppa	Pickles
Mozzarella	Guanciale	Dried figs
Pecorino romano	Pancetta	Pear
Triple cream brie	Chorizo	Whole grain mustard
Provolone	Bresaola	Jam
Drunken goat	Jamon Iberico	Grapes
Langres, champagne washed rind cheese	Mortadella	Honeycrisp apple
Goat Cheese, rolled in freshly minced parsley, thyme + edible flowers	Pepperoni	Marcona almonds
Roomano	Sopressata	Marinated olives
	Speck	Baguette
	Dry-cured sauage	Wafer crackers
		Pretzels

French Onion Soup Flatbread

French Onion Soup has a way of comforting every mouth it meets. It's the kind of soup you can't help but burn your tongue on, because you're too excited to eat it. And the only one that comes with a proper cheese pull, I might add. This recipe gives you all of the same flavors, on top of a buttery, puffed pastry crust.

Makes 2-3 Servings.

2 tablespoons unsalted butter

1 sweet onion, sliced thinly

Pinch of black pepper

1/4 teaspoon sea salt

1/4 cup beef broth

2 tablespoons dry sherry

1 puff pastry sheet, thawed

1 tablespoon olive oil

1 garlic clove, minced

1 cup gruyère cheese, shredded

1/3 cup swiss cheese, shredded

1 tablespoon fresh thyme leaves, for garnish

1. Preheat oven to 400°F.

2. Melt butter over medium heat in a large pan. Add onion and season with salt and pepper. Cook for 7-9 minutes, until they begin to soften.

3. Pour beef broth and sherry into the pan and cook until liquid is almost completely evaporated.

4. Reduce heat to low and cook for 20-25 minutes until onions deepen in color and become jammy. We're setting the stage for perfect caramelization here!

5. Lay thawed puff pastry flat on a baking sheet. Brush pastry with olive oil and minced garlic. Top with onions, gruyère and swiss.

6. Bake for 15-17 minutes. Pull the pastry out when it's kissed with a golden brown color.

7. Garnish with thyme, flaky salt and freshly cracked black pepper.

8. Slice, serve and savor.

Snug's Special Garlic Bread

When you whip up a batch of garlic bread and your entire extended family simultaneously exclaim, "Is this in your cookbook? BECAUSE WE NEED THE RECIPE." You add it into your cookbook. My Aunt Sharon will be especially thrilled.

The specialness of this bread comes from baking it twice and rubbing heaps of roasted garlic into its face. Sexy, I know. Just don't kiss anyone after eating a slice.

Makes 8 Slices.

1 head of garlic, top removed

1 loaf of Italian bread, halved lengthwise

3-4 tablespoons butter, room temperature

1/2 cup parmesan cheese, grated

1/2 teaspoon sea salt

1/4 teaspoon black pepper

1/4 teaspoon parsley flakes

1/4 teaspoon oregano

1/4 teaspoon garlic powder

1/8 cup pecorino cheese

Good olive oil, for drizzling

1. Preheat oven to 400°F.

2. Place garlic on a sheet of aluminum foil. Drizzle with olive oil and wrap the garlic tightly. Roast for 40 minutes. Remove from oven and set aside.

3. Brush the face of each bread half lightly with olive oil. Wrap in aluminum foil and place directly on the middle rack of the oven. Toast for 5-7 minutes, or until a semi-firm crust forms on the bread.

4. Remove bread from oven and use a knife to lather the inside faces with butter. Peel roasted garlic cloves and use your fingers to rub the garlic into the bread. Top with parmesan cheese, salt, pepper, parsley, oregano, garlic powder and pecorino. Drizzle with olive oil.

5. Place garlic bread on a cookie sheet and toast for 2-3 minutes. Broil for an additional 1-2 minutes, or until the edges of the bread are golden brown.

COOKIES, BECAUSE YOU DESERVE THEM

If you're anything like me, you require zero excuses to eat cookies. For those of you with self-control, congratulations. This chapter is for you.

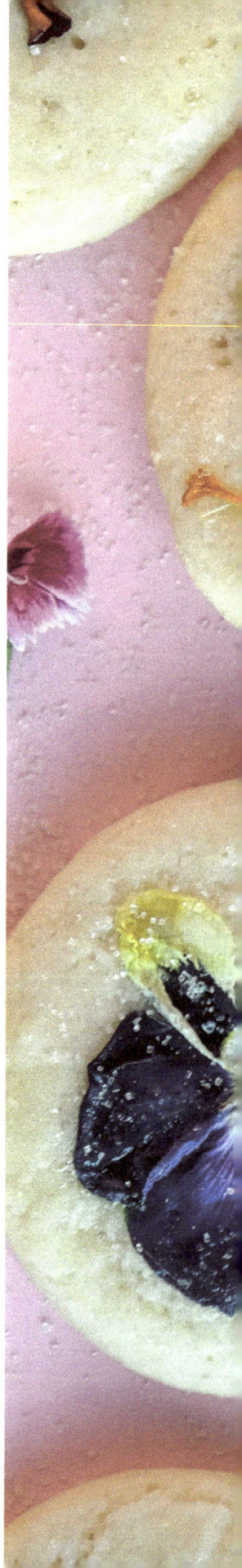

No. 1 Emergency Cookie

It's safe to say there's never a wrong place or time for a cookie. On the flip side, I can think of a million situations when a cookie is 110% required. Like when you wake up to a spiky 7 a.m. email from your boss, or the moment you realize your PMS is in full swing. There are less dramatic situations too - for example, literally any time between breakfast, lunch and dinner. Regardless of the cause for craving, I can tell you this: the No. 1 Emergency Cookie will always come to your rescue.

These cookies are a mecca of the traditional fixings, including coconut flakes, oats and chocolate chips. What takes them the extra mile is a light, crispy cereal called Grape Nut Flakes. If you're scratching your head thinking "what in the.... is that?" imagine a less sweet version of frosted flakes. You'll find these cookies have a delectably chewy center with a crunchy outside. The fact that they don't need any chilling time is an added bonus.

Makes 30 Cookies.

1 cup unsalted butter, room temperature

1/2 cup dark brown sugar

1 cup granulated sugar

3 eggs

1 1/2 teaspoons vanilla

2 cups all-purpose flour

1 teaspoon baking soda

1 1/4 teaspoons baking powder

1 cup grape nut flakes

1 cup organic rolled oats

1 cup unsweetened coconut flakes

6 ounces semi-sweet chocolate chips

1. Preheat oven to 350°F.

2. In a large bowl, use a standing or hand mixer to cream together both sugars and butter.

3. In a separate bowl, whisk together eggs and vanilla. Then mix into the butter and sugar mixture.

4. Next, in another large bowl, whisk together flour, baking soda and baking powder. Gradually mix dry ingredients into the batter, until fully incorporated.

5. Gently fold grape nut flakes, oats, coconut and chocolate chips into the batter.

6. Use an ice cream scoop to drop large dollops of batter onto a greased cookie sheet. Be sure to leave 3 inches in between each cookie.

7. Bake for 10-12 beautiful minutes. Let sit for 5-10 minutes before transferring to a cooling rack.

8. Get your emergency cookie on.

Chocolate Chip Cookies with Sea Salt

Chocolate chip cookies have a way of making you feel at home, no matter where you are. They're notorious for being that warm gooey bite that says, "you're welcome here, stay awhile." And based on the feedback from anyone who's ever tried this recipe, they're highly addicting, too.

There are numerous ways to romanticize chocolate chip cookies, but here's a few additional ways to think about them. Bake these cookies for a friend who needs a mental pick-me-up. Bring them to game night and watch them slowly vanish one by one. Plant them at your desk to make fast friends at work. Use them as a way to say "I'm sorry" when the words refuse to come out. Definitely bake a batch for your sister who just had a baby. Whatever you do, stash a few away for yourself. Trust me, you won't be able to help yourself.

Makes 30 Cookies.

2 3/4 cups all-purpose flour

1/2 teaspoon baking powder

1 1/2 teaspoons baking soda

1/2 teaspoon salt

1 cup unsalted butter, softened

1 1/2 cups light brown sugar, packed

1/2 cup granulated sugar

2 eggs, room temperature

1 tablespoon vanilla extract

1/4 cup maple syrup

2 cups chocolate chips

TIP: Stick a few extra chocolate chips in the top of each cookie just before baking. It's a food styling trick that makes sure each cookie dazzles with gooey chocolate bits.

1. In a large mixing bowl, whisk together flour, baking powder, baking soda and salt. Set aside.

2. Use a standing mixer or hand mixer to cream together butter and sugars in a medium bowl. Mix until light and fluffy, about 2-3 minutes.

3. Add eggs to the mixture. Mix on medium-high until thoroughly combined. Next, add the vanilla and maple syrup.

4. Decrease mixing speed to low and gradually add the dry ingredients. Continue mixing until combined, then fold in chocolate chips.

5. Cover the dough with plastic wrap. Refrigerate for 1 hour.

6. Preheat the oven to 350°F.

7. Remove dough from the refrigerator and roll into 2-inch balls. Place cookies on a parchment lined baking sheet, 1-inch apart.

8. Bake for 10-12 minutes, or until the cookies are light golden.

9. Remove cookies from the oven and cool for 5 minutes before transferring to a cooling rack.

10. Sprinkle with sea salt and serve.

Rainbow Butter Cookies

When I think of butter cookies, my mind ALWAYS goes to Christmas. This recipe belongs to my grandma Connie, and it's coming at you straight from the Bronx, where she grew up. These cookies are little bites of butter cookie bliss, covered in chocolate and dipped in rainbow sprinkles. I'd say the flavors are as big as my grandma's personality, but if I did, I'd be lying.

She's the ultimate Italian grandmother, who talks with her hands and listens with her heart. She's also the reason why our entire family races one another to eat these exact cookies on Christmas eve. I say race, because once they become visible they literally disappear moments later.

Makes 52 Cookies.

1 cup unsalted butter, room temperature

1/2 cup confectioners' sugar

2 cups flour

1 teaspoon vanilla extract

6 ounces chocolate chips

1 tablespoon butter

Rainbow sprinkles

1. In a large bowl, use an electric mixer to beat butter until light and fluffy. Mix in confectioners' sugar, flour and vanilla extract.

2. Use your hands to roll the dough into a ball. Cut the ball in half and wrap each piece in wax paper. Refrigerate for at least 2 hours.

3. Preheat the oven to 350°F.

4. Remove half of the dough from the refrigerator. Use 1 teaspoon to measure and scoop out dough; roll into a two-inch log. Repeat until dough is gone.

5. Bake for 10 to 12 minutes on a parchment-lined baking sheet.

6. While cookies are cooling, melt the chocolate and butter in a double boiler over medium heat. Continuously stir until there are no lumps in the chocolate.

7. Dip the cookies halfway in the melted chocolate, then roll in rainbow sprinkles.

8. Place dipped cookies on a baking sheet lined with wax paper. Cool in the refrigerator.

9. INDULGE.

Coconut Chocolate Chunk Cookies

Sometimes I can't help myself from running to the pantry for a cookie. There, I said it. The first time I baked these bad boys, my boyfriend and I devoured all but two of them in a matter of hours. And guess what? I didn't even think twice about it. Here's why: just like a warm hug from someone you love, you'll never want them to end. And unlike most cookies, you'll never have to feel guilty about eating an entire stick of butter because this batch only uses two tablespoons!

Expect a batch of piping hot chocolate chip cookies with a creamy center, packed with coconut flakes and gooey chocolate chips. These little bites of wonderment are made using almond flour, which is a naturally gluten-free alternative to flour. Pack your bags, we're going on a one-way trip to cookie paradise.

Makes 10 Cookies.

2 tablespoons unsalted butter, room temperature

1/4 cup brown sugar

1 tablespoon vanilla extract

1 large egg, room temperature

2 cups almond flour, blanched or raw

1/4 teaspoon salt

1/2 teaspoon baking soda

1/4 teaspoon baking powder

1/2 cup semi-sweet chocolate chips

1/3 cup unsweetened coconut flakes

Maldon salt, to garnish

1. Preheat the oven to 350°F.

2. In a medium sized bowl, use a standing mixer or hand mixer to beat together sugar and butter. Beat until mixture is light in color and fluffy.

3. Mix in vanilla and egg until incorporated.

4. In a small bowl, whisk together almond flour, salt, baking soda and baking powder. Mix dry ingredients into wet ingredients in sections, until fully incorporated. Don't forget to scrape your batter down the sides of the bowl.

5. Fold in chocolate chips and coconut flakes.

6. Use an ice cream scoop to drop dough onto a parchment-lined baking sheet. Repeat until your batter is gone.

7. Use the bottom of a wine glass to gently flatten the top of each cookie. They will hardly expand on their own! I like to keep mine about half-inch thick.

8. Bake for 9-10 minutes. Remove from oven and allow cookies to set for 2 minutes. Then transfer to a cooling rack.

9. Finish with a generous sprinkle of Maldon salt.

Sugar Cookies with Bergamot Edible Flowers

Sugar cookies are notorious for being the blank canvas of desserts. They constantly put up with us transforming them into snowflakes, anti-Valentine's day conversation hearts and any cookie cutter shape we can get our hands on (literally). They've proved to be the most versatile treat of our time, and for that, we should be thankful. You'll be extra grateful after you bake your way through this recipe, especially if you love bergamot.

To me, bergamot was destined to be paired with our darling friend, the sugar cookie. It's citrusy and tart with light spicy notes. Understated elegance in one delicate whiff. A wondrous guest at any aromatic party. The cat's flavor meow. Prepare yourself for a chewy, fragrant sugar cookie that's all dressed up with nowhere to go... except your stomach.

Makes 25-30 Cookies.

COOKIES

2 1/2 cups all-purpose flour

1 tablespoon baking powder

1/2 teaspoon salt

1 cup unsalted butter, softened

1 cup granulated sugar

1 large egg, room temperature

1 large egg white, room temperature

2 tablespoons sour cream

1 1/2 teaspoons vanilla extract

1-2 drops of bergamot essential oil

Edible flowers, to garnish

ICING

2 cups confectioners' sugar

1 teaspoon clear vanilla extract

2 tablespoons whole milk

1. In a large mixing bowl, whisk flour, baking powder and salt together. Set aside.

2. Use a standing mixer to cream together butter and sugar in a medium bowl. Mix until it's light and soft. Add eggs to the sugar and butter, mixing until thoroughly combined. Next, mix in sour cream and vanilla.

3. Add the dry ingredients, gradually. Use a rubber spatula to scrape dough down the sides of the bowl. Mix in essential oil.

4. Use your hands to shape the cookie dough into a 3-inch tall log and wrap tightly with wax paper. Refrigerate for at least 2 hours. You can leave the cookies in the fridge for up to 5 days.

5. When you're ready to bake, preheat the oven to 350°F. Use a knife to cut quarter-inch cookie slices and place on a greased baking sheet, 2 inches apart.

6. Bake for 7-9 minutes, or until the edges of the cookies start to bronze. The top of each one should remain pale, like a sugary Snow White.

7. Remove cookies from the oven and cool for 5-10 minutes before transferring to a cooling rack. To make the icing, whisk together confectioners' sugar, vanilla and milk in a small bowl. You're looking for a smooth, creamy consistency. If it's too runny, add more confectioners' sugar.

8. When cookies reach room temperature, ice and garnish with dried or fresh edible flower petals.

Double Chocolate Slam Cookies

Chocolate will forever remind me of my dad. When I was 5 and 6 years old, I had a glorious habit of sneaking downstairs before anyone else was awake to watch my favorite TV shows. The Ninja Turtles and Saved by the Bell were my top picks. Waking up early also meant I could catch my dad before he left for work. We had our own little ritual. He would stir me up an icy glass of chocolate milk and I'd give him the biggest hug ever before he walked out the door. Looking back, I was one lucky girl.

Aside from taking me down a sweet, Willy Wonka version of memory lane, these cookies are soft, chewy and hella chocolaty. They're also the perfect stress-reliever after a long day. *Disclaimer: Slamming a tray of cookies on the counter is just as fun as it sounds.* Eat them with a glass of red wine or your favorite non-dairy milk. You deserve them, either way.

Makes 18 Cookies.

1 1/4 cups unsalted butter, room temperature

1 cup granulated sugar

1/2 cup brown sugar, packed

1 large egg, room temperature

2 large egg yolks, room temperature

2 teaspoons vanilla extract

1/2 cup unsweetened cocoa powder

2 cups all-purpose flour

1 1/2 teaspoons baking powder

1/4 cup cocoa nibs

1/4 teaspoon kosher salt

2 tablespoons milk

1 cup semi-sweet chocolate chunks

1. In a medium bowl, use a standing or hand mixer to cream butter and sugar together on medium speed.

2. Add the egg, egg yolks, and vanilla. Mix until combined.

3. In a separate bowl, sift together cocoa, flour, baking powder, nibs and salt. Then gradually add dry ingredients into the batter. Finish by mixing in milk.

4. Fold in the chocolate chunks.

5. Cover the dough bowl tightly. Refrigerate for 1 hour.

6. Preheat the oven to 375˚F.

7. Use a 1/4 cup measuring cup to scoop and roll dough into a ball. Place cookies on a parchment-lined cookie sheet, leaving at least 3 inches in between each.

8. Bake for 10 minutes, or until the cookies are set around the edges but soft in the middle.

9. As soon as you remove the cookies from the oven, slam the cookie sheet on the counter (really hard!) repeatedly, until cracks form in the tops of the cookies. Let the cookies sit on the sheet for 5-7 minutes before transferring to a cooling rack.

10. Top with Maldon salt and appease your inner cookie monster.

UNBIRTHDAY CAKES

It seems unfair that your birthday is the only day of the entire year when you can blow out candles standing in a cake. These cakes are for the person who wants to make a wish every day, followed by a mouthful of delicious dessert. Life just got a whole lot sweeter.

Cardamom Rose Pudding Cake

This recipe marries two of my favorite desserts: cake and pudding. There's a priest, flower girl, the coming together of two sweethearts sealed with a kiss... the whole deal. Just kidding, but this pudding cake does make a smashing entrance. No white dress necessary.

It behaves similarly to a soufflé in the sense that it's light, dreamy and sophisticated. The moment you softly dig into the bottom of your dessert dish, your spoon will push through an airy cake only to strike pudding gold. I feel like this recipe is what the heart-eyed emoji would taste like if you could eat it. Falling in like at first bite is a real thing. As they say, the proof is in the pudding.

Makes 6 Servings.

6 green cardamom pods, crushed

1 1/3 cups milk (2% or whole)

1/2 cup sugar

1/3 cup all-purpose flour

1/4 teaspoon salt

3 eggs, room temperature + separated

2 tablespoons unsalted butter, melted

1/2 teaspoon rose water

1 teaspoon lemon zest, grated

1 tablespoon vanilla extract

Confectioners' sugar, for garnish

1. Preheat the oven to 350°F. Then grease an 8-inch pie dish with nonstick spray and set aside.

2. Use a rolling pin or mortar and pestle to crush the cardamom pods open.

3. In a small pot, heat milk and cardamom over medium heat. Once the milk begins to simmer, remove from heat and let steep for 10-15 minutes. When ready, strain and set aside.

4. In a medium bowl, whisk 1/4 cup of sugar with flour and salt until combined.

5. In a separate bowl, whisk egg yolks, melted butter, infused milk, rose water, zest and vanilla extract. Then whisk wet ingredients into dry ingredients until well blended.

6. Use a standing or hand mixer to beat egg whites and remaining 1/4 cup of sugar in a large bowl, until stiff peaks form. When the whites become glossy, use a rubber spatula to gently fold egg whites into the cake batter. The batter should be fluffy and cloudlike, but smooth.

7. Pour batter into prepared pie dish.

8. Fill the bottom of a sheet pan with 1 1/2-inch of water. Place pie dish in water bath. Bake for 30-35 minutes, until the cake is light golden.

9. Remove from oven and transfer to a cooling rack. Serve warm or at room temperature. Top with a scoop of vanilla ice cream or confectioners' sugar, if you're feeling extra.

Piña Colada Icebox Cake

If you like Piña Coladas and eating cake every day.
If you're not into yoga, and you have half a brain.
If you like making love at midnight, or a kitchen escape,
This is the love that you've looked for, and it's in a frozen cake.

I hope you sung that entire verse in your head, and if you didn't, you'll be in the mood to soon. A traditional icebox cake consists of layered whipped cream and thin cookies. This recipe is my version of a boozy, icebox cake modeled after one of my favorite frozen cocktails. The infused whipped cream has a modest rum flavor, but taste as you go and add more if you fancy a double shot kind of vibe.

Makes 8 Servings.

2 1/2 cups heavy whipping cream

1/2 cup confectioners' sugar

1 tablespoon vanilla extract

1/2 cup pineapple juice

2 tablespoons rum

2/3 cup cream of coconut

1 sleeve of graham crackers

1/4 cup unsweetened coconut flakes, toasted

Maraschino cherries, for garnish

1. In the bowl of an electric mixer, whip heavy whipping cream, confectioners' sugar and vanilla extract until stiff.

2. Use a rubber spatula to gently fold in pineapple juice, rum and coconut cream.

3. In a round 9-inch springform pan, layer one-third of the whipped cream in the bottom of the pan and top with graham crackers. Add another layer of whipped cream, then graham crackers. Finish with another layer of whipped cream.

4. Garnish the top of the cake with toasted coconut flakes and cherries.

5. Cover and freeze for 3-4 hours.

6. When ready to serve, remove the springform and slice.

Grandma's Cheesecake

It feels like I should tell you that I don't love cheesecake. In fact, I don't like cheesecake even a little bit... unless it's my grandma Connie's recipe.

I decided to give this classic dessert a second, third and fourth chance, the moment my grandmother told me too. I don't know if anyone reading this has an Italian grandmother, but if you do, you know that refusing to eat something they've prepared is basically a sin. The first time she casually made cheesecake in front of me, I remember taking mental note of the sweet mise en place. One spring pan accompanied by several blocks of cream cheese resting next to heaps of sugar; all waiting to be formally introduced to each other. My seven-year-old eyes were as wide as ever, in anticipation. When I realized it needed to bake and then chill for three hours, it was almost like being sentenced to dessert jail.

The texture of the filling is the first thing you'll appreciate when you bite into this cake. It's wonderfully creamy, yet firm enough to stand sweetly on its own. Then there's the homemade, buttery graham cracker crust. Trust me, all you need is one forkful to know why this cake is close to my heart and taste buds.

Makes 8 Servings.

CRUST

1 1/2 sleeves of graham crackers, crushed finely

4 tablespoons unsalted butter, melted

1 1/2 tablespoons sugar

FILLING

24 ounces cream cheese

1 1/2 cups fine granulated sugar

6 eggs

16 ounces sour cream

2 tablespoons vanilla extract

1. Preheat oven to 375°F. Grease a 9-inch springform pan. Set aside.

2. Use a food processor or rolling pin to crush graham crackers into fine crumbs. Transfer to a small bowl and use your hands to mix in butter and sugar. Once combined, press crust mixture evenly into the bottom of the prepared pan.

3. In a large bowl, beat cream cheese on medium speed, until soft and creamy. Mix in sugar, adding 1/4 cup at a time. Beat in eggs, one at a time, just until combined. Lastly, add sour cream and vanilla to the mixture. Mix well. There should be zero lumps, y'all.

4. Create a water bath for the cheesecake by filling a roasting pan with 2 inches of water. Wrap aluminum foil around the springform pan and place in water bath. Pour cheesecake batter over graham cracker crust.

5. Bake on the middle rack of oven for 35 minutes. When ready, leave the cake in the oven for one hour. Don't open the door - the heat will escape!

6. Remove the cake from the oven and water bath; transfer to a to cooling rack. When the cake reaches room temperature, refrigerate for at least 3 hours prior to serving.

The Best Chocolate Cake

My ideal cake is light, fluffy and tastes so good that I physically can't stop eating it. This chocolate cake checks all of those boxes, especially when it's covered in a vanilla buttercream frosting.

As far as what you should know about the recipe, expect the batter to be really thin and runny. Don't fret, that's exactly how it's meant to be. If you don't have buttermilk in your fridge, just stir 1 tablespoon of lemon juice into milk; let it sit for 5 minutes until the milk begins to curdle; use in the recipe. This really is the best chocolate cake ever.

Makes 8 Servings.

CAKE

2 cups granulated sugar

2 cups cake flour

3/4 cup unsweetened cocoa powder

1 1/2 teaspoons baking powder

1 teaspoon baking soda

1 teaspoon salt

2 large eggs

1/2 cup vegetable oil

1 cup buttermilk

2 teaspoons vanilla extract

1 cup freshly brewed coffee

1/8 cup cocoa nibs

VANILLA BUTTERCREAM

2 1/2 cups unsalted butter, softened

2 tablespoons vanilla extract

6 cups confectioners' sugar

5-6 tablespoons heavy cream

1. Preheat the oven to 350°F.

2. Sift together sugar, flour, cocoa powder, baking powder, baking soda and salt in a medium sized bowl.

3. In a separate bowl, use a hand or standing mixer to combine eggs, oil, buttermilk and vanilla.

4. Add dry ingredients in sections, about 1/2 cup at a time. When completely incorporated, reduce your mixer speed to the lowest setting and gradually mix in hot coffee. Fold in cocoa nibs.

5. Pour into two parchment lined 8-inch baking pans.

6. Bake for 35-40 minutes. Use a toothpick to test the cakes - if the toothpick comes out clean, the cakes are done. Remove from the oven and cool.

7. For the buttercream, use a mixer to beat the butter until light and airy, about 3 minutes. Mix in vanilla and sugar until incorporated, then add heavy cream. Continue to beat the buttercream until it's silky and sultry.

8. When the cakes have cooled to room temperature, frost your little heart out.

Strawberry Tart

If you've never danced down rows of brazen strawberry bushes, you truly haven't lived yet. Growing up in Upstate New York, I was lucky enough to have strawberries in my backyard. Unfortunately for everyone else in my family, I was really good at secretly popping them into my mouth before they had the chance to pick them. What can I say? I've always had a competitive streak, especially when there's food involved.

This recipe takes me on an adventure that smells like summer and tastes even better. You might find yourself forming a love-hate relationship with this strawberry tart. Mainly because once you start eating it, it's hard to stop. It's jammy, fragrant and the crust melts in your mouth. This tart is also an absolutely perfect addition to any picnic or outing in the sunshine. Stick a candle in it for a unique way to host a birthday celebration. I promise, whoever has the opportunity to try this tart will thank you.

Makes 8 Servings.

CRUST

1/2 cup confectioners' sugar

1 1/2 cups all-purpose flour

1/4 teaspoon salt

1 1/2 sticks unsalted butter, softened + sliced

FILLING

4 cups strawberries, tops removed, sliced in halves + quarters

3/4 cup sugar

3 tablespoons cornstarch

1 teaspoon cinnamon

1 teaspoon lemon juice

1. Preheat oven to 400°F.

2. In a medium bowl, combine confectioners' sugar, flour, salt and butter. Use your hands to knead the ingredients into a dough. It'll be crumbly at first, but will come together! Roll dough into a ball.

3. Generously flour a piece of wax paper and place it on your counter. Use a rolling pin to roll out the tart dough on a piece of wax paper, until it's a 1/4 inch thick.

4. Flip the wax paper over to transfer the dough into a 9-inch spring pan or pie dish. The crust should be 1-2 inches tall up the sides of the dish.

5. In a separate bowl, combine strawberries with sugar, cornstarch, cinnamon and lemon juice. Gently stir to coat berries thoroughly.

6. Pour strawberry filling into the prepared pie crust.

7. Bake for 1 hour. Remove from oven and let sit for 25 minutes.

8. Slice and eat!

Earl Grey Tea Cake with Cream Cheese Frosting

For as long as I can remember, my mother has maintained a healthy stash of Earl Grey tea in the pantry. It's been an essential after dinner digestive and before bedtime elixir, and today it's becoming your new favorite unbirthday cake.

If you've never had the pleasure of sipping this tea, it's a blend of black tea infused with citrusy pops of bergamot. By steeping the tea leaves into milk, this tiered cake takes on a delicate, fragrant taste with a fluffy texture. The cream cheese frosting is the proverbial cherry on top of this high tea inspired cake. Pinky's up, friends!

Makes 8 Servings.

CAKE

1 cup milk

2 earl grey tea bags

2 1/2 cups cake flour

1/2 teaspoon salt

2 teaspoons baking powder

1 teaspoon baking soda

1/2 teaspoon ground earl grey tea leaves

3/4 cup unsalted butter, room temperature

1 1/2 cups sugar

3 eggs, room temperature

1 tablespoon vanilla extract

Zest of 1 lemon

FROSTING

8 ounces cream cheese

1/2 stick unsalted butter, room temperature

3 cups confectioners' sugar

2 teaspoons vanilla extract

Pinch salt

1. Preheat oven to 350°F.

2. Heat milk over medium heat in a small pot. Bring to a boil. Place 2 tea bags of earl grey tea in the milk. Immediately remove from heat and set aside to steep for 5 minutes.

3. In a large bowl, whisk cake flour, salt, baking powder, baking soda and ground tea leaves until combined.

4. In a separate bowl, use a hand or standing mixer to cream butter and sugar together. Add eggs, one at a time. Then stir in vanilla and lemon zest.

5. Mix dry ingredients into the batter in sections. Scraping down sides of the bowl occasionally to ensure it's fully incorporated.

6. Reduce mixer speed to low and gradually add the tea infused milk.

7. Scoop batter into two prepared 9-inch cake pans. Bake for 30 minutes. Stick a toothpick in the cake to test it for doneness. When the toothpick comes out clean, your cake is ready. *HOORAY* Transfer to cooling rack and cool.

8. Meanwhile, in a large mixing bowl, cream together cream cheese and butter on medium speed. Reduce speed and beat in confectioners' sugar, one cup at a time. Once incorporated, add in vanilla and salt.

9. When the cake reaches room temperature, frost away! Top with fresh berries, if you please.

Acknowledgments

Is it weird that I've been thinking about the acknowledgment section of this cookbook since the VERY beginning? Never did I ever think I would write, photograph, style and design an entire cookbook. What's more impressive is all the friends I've made along the way. I truly have so much to be thankful for.

I'd like to start by celebrating and thanking my mother, Susan, and father, Ralph, who have always supported and believed in me, even when I was incapable of believing in myself. You've surrounded me in a place of love for as long as I can remember. Your encouragement throughout this cookbook journey was no different. You never stopped answering my phone calls, even though half of them featured me, hysterically crying about things I can't recall now. You are the best parents in the world - and I love making you proud!

To my sister, Stephanie, and her husband, Robby, thank you for always sharing my enthusiasm for food. I love cooking with you, dancing around the kitchen holding raw turkeys by the wings on Thanksgiving, and laughing our asses off while reverse-searing $80 steaks. You make my heart wildly happy.

A gigantic warm thank you to my entire extended family for filling my childhood with more Italian food, hugs and laughter than I could have ever hoped for. It's still the only cuisine I'll never tire of. Largely because it reminds me of all the memories I have with you. I hope that seeing your recipes in this book reminds you of how special you are.

I am beyond grateful for my time and mentors in New York City, especially at Neuman's Kitchen Events & Catering. Stacy Pearl, Robb Garceau, Paul Neuman and the entire culinary team. I learned so much from you in the kitchen, at menu photoshoots with Jen May and during our tasting field trips in the city. Chef-guided walking tours through Chinatown markets, eating our way through Michelin Star restaurants in the Lower East Side, dreaming up menus for New York's finest events and humans... Ah, the time I spent working at NK as the Director of Marketing is an era I'll cherish forever.

This book wouldn't have been possible without my friends. Titi, Emily, Jacklyn, Samantha, Christi, Gina, Alexandra -- you girls redefined the meaning of friendship for me through your genuine support, endless food banter and unwavering willingness to be taste testers. The support I received from friends and total strangers alike, was incredibly humbling. It reminded me that there are tons of wonderful people in the world, waiting to be embraced.

Thank you to everyone who called to check in when I was running around my apartment holding a 3-foot tall reflector in one hand and my Fujifilm camera in the other, and was seemingly nowhere to be found. All of your calls, texts and encouragement throughout the creation of this book meant a lot to me. It's a piece of my heart, truly!

Thank you to Corningware and Dream Farm, who hooked me up with cooking gear and gadgets when I was knee-deep in the process.

Lastly, thank you to whoever is reading this right now. Thank you for investing your time, money and love for food in this book, and in me. I appreciate you!

Meet the Author

Melissa Santell is a native New Yorker with a serious love for eating, reading her Aquarian horoscope and food photography.

She founded her company, FoodxFeels, in 2017, as a space to create better conversations around the one thing we literally can't live without: food. Today, it's a photography + strategic marketing studio that gives food brands the recognition they deserve. Because good food should be seen, experienced and tasted!

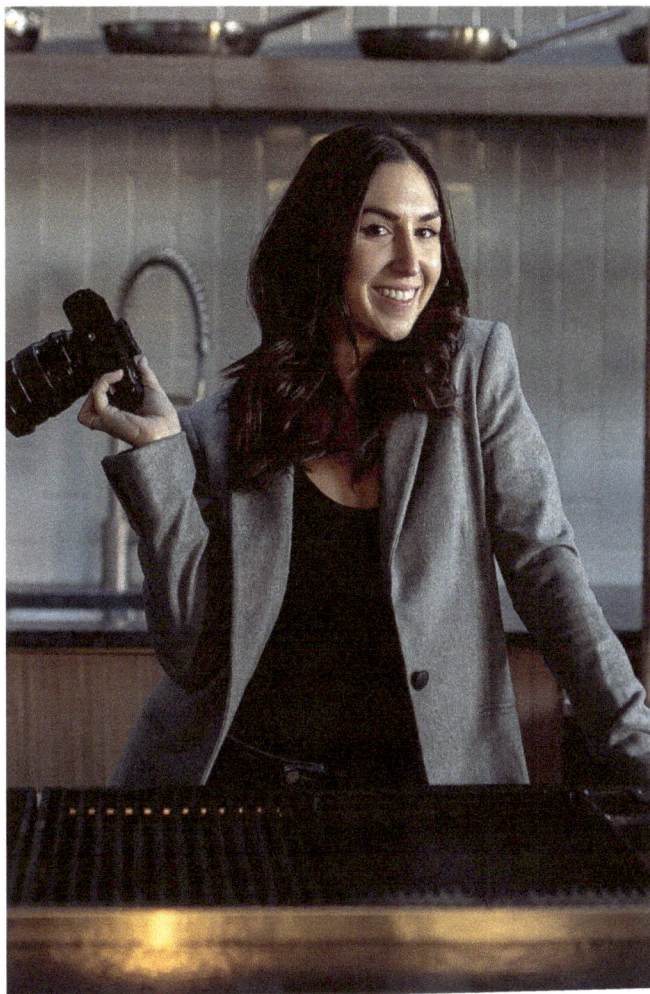

When Melissa isn't snapping photos of new client menus or repping brands on Channel 8 News, you can find her digging into the closest budino.

To follow along with her craving-driven musings, visit www.foodxfeels.com or say hello on Instagram at @melsantell.

www.ingramcontent.com/pod-product-compliance
Lightning Source LLC
Chambersburg PA
CBHW040315100426

42811CB00012B/1450